Teach Yourself
VISUALLY™
Macs
2nd Edition

Visual

by Paul McFedries

WILEY

Wiley Publishing Inc.

Teach Yourself VISUALLY™ Macs, 2nd Edition

Published by
Wiley Publishing, Inc.
10475 Crosspoint Boulevard
Indianapolis, IN 46256

www.wiley.com

Published simultaneously in Canada

Library of Congress Control Number: 2010933464

ISBN: 978-0-470-88848-3

Manufactured in the United States of America

10 9 8 7 6 5 4 3 2 1

Trademark Acknowledgments

Contact Us

For general information on our other products and services please contact our Customer Care Department within the U.S. at 877-762-2974, outside the U.S. at 317-572-3993, or fax 317-572-4002.

For technical support please visit www.wiley.com/techsupport.

Wiley Publishing, Inc.

Sales

Contact Wiley
at (877) 762-2974 or
fax (317) 572-4002.

Credits

Acquisitions Editor
Aaron Black

Project Editor
Lynn Northrup

Technical Editor
Dennis Cohen

Editorial Director
Robyn Siesky

Editorial Manager
Rosemarie Graham

Business Manager
Amy Knies

Senior Marketing Manager
Sandy Smith

Vice President and Executive Group Publisher
Richard Swadley

Vice President and Executive Publisher
Barry Pruett

Project Coordinator
Patrick Redmond

Graphics and Production Specialists
Andrea Hornberger
Jennifer Mayberry

Quality Control Technicians
Melissa Cossell
Rob Springer

Proofreader
Susan Hobbs

Indexer
Christine Karpeles

Screen Artist
Jill A. Proll

Illustrators
Ronda David-Burroughs
Cheryl Grubbs

About the Author

Paul McFedries is is a technical writer who has been authoring computer books since 1991. He has more than 70 books to his credit, which together have sold more than three million copies worldwide. These books include the Wiley titles *Teach Yourself VISUALLY Microsoft Office 2008 for Mac, Teach Yourself VISUALLY Mac OS X Snow Leopard*, and *Macs Portable Genius*. Paul also runs Word Spy, a Web site dedicated to tracking new words and phrases (see www.wordspy.com). Please visit Paul's personal Web site at www.mcfedries.com.

Author's Acknowledgments

The book you hold in your hands is not only an excellent learning tool, but it is truly beautiful, as well. I am happy to have supplied the text that you will read, but the gorgeous images come from Wiley's crack team of artists and illustrators. The layout of the tasks, the accuracy of the spelling and grammar, and the veracity of the information are all the result of hard work performed by project editor Lynn Northrup and technical editor Dennis Cohen. Thanks to both of you for your excellent work. My thanks, as well, to acquisitions editor Aaron Black for asking me to write this book.

How to Use This Book

Who This Book Is For

This book is for the reader who has never used this particular technology or software application. It is also for readers who want to expand their knowledge.

The Conventions in This Book

① Steps

This book uses a step-by-step format to guide you easily through each task. Numbered steps are actions you must do; bulleted steps clarify a point, step, or optional feature; and indented steps give you the result.

② Notes

Notes give additional information — special conditions that may occur during an operation, a situation that you want to avoid, or a cross-reference to a related area of the book.

③ Icons and Buttons

Icons and buttons show you exactly what you need to click to perform a step.

④ Tips

Tips offer additional information, including warnings and shortcuts.

⑤ Bold

Bold type shows command names, options, and text or numbers you must type.

⑥ Italics

Italic type introduces and defines a new term.

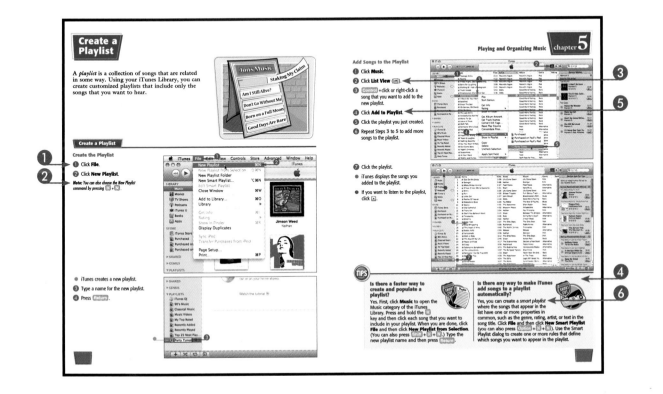

Table of Contents

chapter 1   Learning About Mac Types

chapter 2   Understanding What You Can Do with Your Mac

chapter 3 Connecting Devices to Your Mac

chapter 4 Learning Mac Basics

Table of Contents

chapter 5   Playing and Organizing Music

chapter 6   Viewing and Editing Your Photos

chapter 7 Playing and Creating Digital Video

Table of Contents

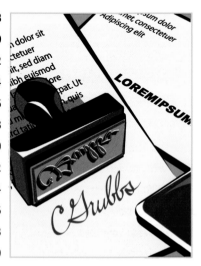

chapter 10 Tracking Your Contacts and Events

chapter 11 Working with Your MobileMe Account

Table of Contents

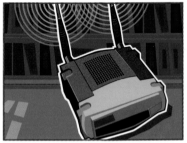

chapter **14** Maintaining Your Mac

chapter **15** Troubleshooting Your Mac

CHAPTER 1

Learning About Mac Types

Are you ready to learn about the Mac? This chapter gets you off to a great start by showing you the different types of Macs that are available. You learn about the general Mac types and find out about the specific Mac models and what features they offer.

Understanding Mac Types

Before you learn about the specific Mac models Apple offers, it is a good idea to take a step back and look at the general types of Macs that are available.

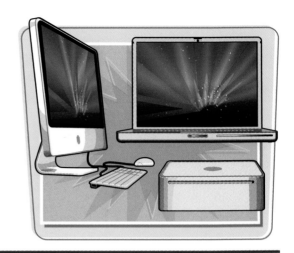

Desktop Macs

A desktop Mac is a Macintosh computer that is designed to sit on your desk. In most cases, you connect the desktop Mac to a separate keyboard, mouse, and monitor. The exception here is the iMac model, which comes with a built-in monitor. Also, the Mac Pro model is quite large, so many people place the system unit on the floor.

Portable Macs

A portable Mac is a Macintosh computer that you can take with you when you leave your home or office. A portable Mac — also called a laptop or notebook Mac — comes with a keyboard, mouse, and monitor built in, so it is easy to use in almost any location. A portable Mac also comes with a battery, so you can use it even in places where there is no power outlet available.

PowerPC Macs

From about 1994 to early 2006, all Mac models used a central processing unit (CPU; the "brain" of the computer) called the PowerPC, which was made jointly by IBM and Motorola. Apple no longer uses PowerPC CPUs, but if you are in the market for a used Mac, note that it may come with the PowerPC chip.

Intel Macs

All of the current Mac models use a CPU made by Intel Corporation. Apple began the transition from PowerPC to Intel in 2006, and every Mac made since about August 2006 comes with an Intel CPU. The Intel processors are faster than the PowerPC chips, and they use less power, which improves battery life in portable Macs.

Determine the Mac CPU

If you have a Mac and you do not know whether it has an Intel or PowerPC CPU, you can find out. Start your Mac, click the Apple icon (⬛) in the top left corner, and then click **About This Mac**. In the About This Mac window that appears, examine the Processor value.

Learn About the iMac

If you are thinking of purchasing an iMac, or just want to know more about this Mac model, this section explains the iMac's features and concepts.

iMac Overview

The iMac is an "all-in-one" computer that combines the system components (the CPU, memory, hard drive, and other internal components) and the screen in a single unit. The resulting console is amazingly thin, so the iMac does not take up very much room on your desk.

iMac Features

The iMac uses an Intel Core i3, Intel Core i5, or Intel Core i7 processor; a widescreen display (21.5 or 27 inches wide); a powerful graphics card; a built-in iSight camera and microphone; wired and wireless networking support; and a CD and DVD burner.

iMac Ports

The back of the iMac has a generous supply of ports that enable you to connect a wide variety of devices.

Audio Out

You use the audio out port to play music or other audio through speakers or headphones.

Audio In

You use the audio in port to bring speech or other audio into the iMac using a microphone, musical instrument, or audio player.

USB

You use the iMac's four USB ports to connect devices that support USB, including keyboards, mice, printers, cameras, external drives, iPods, iPads, and iPhones.

FireWire 800

You use the FireWire 800 port to connect devices that support FireWire 800 or FireWire 400 (with an adapter), including external hard drives, external DVD drives, and video cameras.

Mini DisplayPort Out

You use this video out port to connect the iMac to an additional display, such as a second monitor, a TV, or a video projector.

Network

You use the network port to connect the iMac to a wired network.

Delve into the Mac Mini

If you are thinking of purchasing a Mac mini, or just want to know more about this Mac model, this section explains the Mac mini's features and concepts.

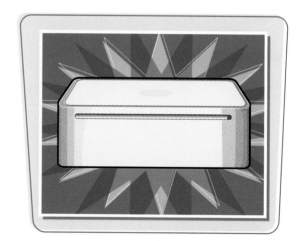

Mac Mini Overview

The Mac mini is a scaled-down version of a Mac that includes all the standard components — CPU, memory, hard drive, video card, and DVD drive — in a unit that measures only about 6.5 inches square (and about 2 inches tall). This makes the Mac mini perfect for a small work area.

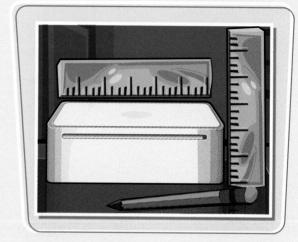

Mac Mini Features

The Mac mini uses an Intel Core 2 Duo processor; a 320GB or 500GB hard drive; wired and wireless networking support; a CD and DVD burner; and numerous ports (see the next page). You need to supply your own keyboard, mouse, and monitor.

Mac Mini Ports

The back of the Mac mini has a number of ports that enable you to connect a wide variety of devices.

Network

You use the network port to connect the Mac mini to a wired network.

FireWire 800

You use the FireWire 800 port to connect devices that support FireWire 800 or FireWire 400 (with an adapter), including external hard drives, external DVD drives, and video cameras.

HDMI Video Out

You use the HDMI video out port to connect the Mac mini to an HD TV or other display that uses an HDMI connector.

Mini DisplayPort Video Out

You use the Mini DisplayPort video out port to connect the Mac mini to a high resolution display.

USB

You use the Mac mini's USB ports to connect devices that support USB, including keyboards, mice, printers, cameras, external drives, iPods, iPads, and iPhones.

Audio In

You use the audio in port to bring speech or other audio into the Mac mini using a microphone, musical instrument, or audio player.

Audio Out

You use the audio out port to play music or other audio through speakers or headphones.

If you are thinking of purchasing a Mac Pro, or just want to know more about this Mac model, this section explains the Mac Pro's features and concepts.

Mac Pro Overview

The Mac Pro is the fastest and most powerful of all the Mac models. With a fast CPU, lots of memory, a large hard drive, powerful graphics, and a wide variety of expansion options, the Mac Pro is designed for power users who need maximum performance and expandability.

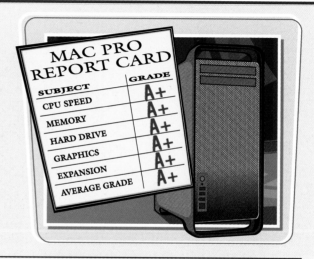

MAC PRO REPORT CARD

SUBJECT	GRADE
CPU SPEED	A+
MEMORY	A+
HARD DRIVE	A+
GRAPHICS	A+
EXPANSION	A+
AVERAGE GRADE	A+

Mac Pro Features

The Mac Pro uses either one or two Intel Xeon quad core processors, which gives the Mac Pro the power of up to eight individual CPUs, or two Intel Xeon 6-core processors, which is the equivalent of 12 individual CPUs. It also comes with 3GB or 6GB of memory, a 1TB hard drive, wired and optional wireless networking support, a CD and DVD burner, and numerous ports. You can upgrade the Mac Pro with a faster CPU, more memory, and multiple hard drives.

MAC PRO
• INTEL XEON QUAD CORE PROCESSORS
• 3GB OF MEMORY
• 1TB HARD DRIVE
• WIRED AND WIRELESS NETWORK SUPPORT
• CD AND DVD BURNER

Mac Pro Ports

The back of the Mac Pro has a number of ports that enable you to connect a wide variety of devices. Note that the Mac Pro also has several ports on the front.

DVI Video Out

You use the DVI video out port to connect the Mac Pro to a computer monitor, TV, or other display.

Mini DisplayPort Video Out

You use the Mini DisplayPort video out port to connect the Mac Pro to a high resolution display.

USB

You use the Mac Pro's three USB ports to connect devices that support USB, including keyboards, mice, printers, cameras, external drives, and iPods.

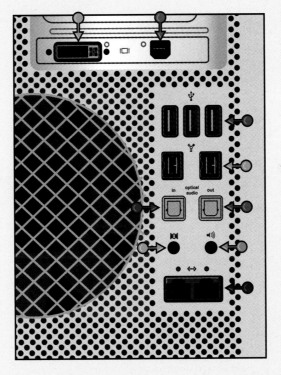

Audio Out

You use the audio out port to play music or other audio through speakers or headphones.

FireWire 800

You use the two FireWire 800 ports to connect devices that support FireWire 800 or FireWire 400 (with an adapter), including external hard drives, external DVD drives, and video cameras.

Network

You can use the two network ports to connect the Mac Pro to two different wired networks.

Optical Audio In

You use the optical audio in port to bring digital audio into the Mac Pro using digital audio devices that support optical connections.

Optical Audio Out

You use the optical audio out port to send digital audio from the Mac Pro to digital audio devices that support optical connections.

Audio In

You use the audio in port to bring speech or other audio into the Mac Pro using a microphone, musical instrument, or audio player.

Check Out the MacBook Pro

If you are thinking of purchasing a MacBook Pro, or just want to know more about this Mac model, this section explains the MacBook Pro's features and concepts.

MacBook Pro Overview

The MacBook Pro is a portable computer that combines the monitor and keyboard into a single unit. Instead of a mouse, the MacBook Pro uses a trackpad where you move the pointer by sliding your finger along the pad. The latest MacBook Pro models use Multi-Touch trackpads, where you use gestures to scroll, rotate, and zoom screen objects.

- Intel Core 2 Duo processor
- Widescreen display
- 4GB of memory
- 250GB or 500GB hard drive
- iSight camera and microphone
- Wire & wireless network support
- CD & DVD burner

MacBook Pro Features

The MacBook Pro uses an Intel Core 2 Duo processor; a widescreen display (13, 15, or 17 inches measured diagonally); 4GB of memory; a 250GB, 320GB, or 500GB hard drive; a built-in iSight camera and microphone; wired and wireless networking support; and a CD and DVD burner.

MacBook Pro Ports

The sides of the MacBook Pro have a number of ports that enable you to connect a wide variety of devices. Note that the different versions of the MacBook (13-, 15-, and 17-inch) have slightly different port configurations. A 15-inch MacBook Pro is shown here.

Network

You use the network port to connect the MacBook Pro to a wired network.

FireWire 800

You use the FireWire 800 port to connect devices that support FireWire 800 or FireWire 400 (with an adapter), including external hard drives, external DVD drives, and video cameras.

Mini DisplayPort Video Out

You use the Mini DisplayPort video out port to connect the MacBook Pro to an additional display, such as a second monitor, a TV, or a video projector.

USB

You use the MacBook Pro's USB ports to connect devices that support USB, including keyboards, mice, printers, cameras, external drives, and iPods.

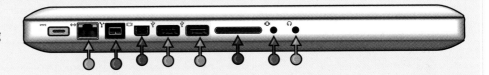

SD Card Slot

You use the SD card slot to insert a Secure Digital memory card.

Audio In

You use the audio in port to bring speech or other audio into the MacBook Pro using a microphone, musical instrument, or audio player.

Audio Out

You use the audio out port to play music or other audio through speakers or headphones.

If you are thinking of purchasing a MacBook Air, or just want to know more about this Mac model, this section explains the MacBook Air's features and concepts.

MacBook Air Overview

The MacBook Air is a portable computer that combines the monitor and keyboard into a single unit. Instead of a mouse, the MacBook Air uses a Multi-Touch trackpad where you move the pointer by sliding your finger along the pad, and where you use gestures to scroll, rotate, and zoom screen objects. With a height of just 0.76 inches, the MacBook Air is the world's thinnest notebook computer.

MacBook Air News!

FEATURES:
Intel Core 2 Duo processor
13.3-inch widescreen display
2GB of memory
120GB hard drive
iSight camera & microphone
Wireless network support

MacBook Air Features

The MacBook Air uses an Intel Core 2 Duo processor, a 13.3-inch widescreen display (measured diagonally), 2GB of memory, a 120GB hard drive, a built-in iSight camera and microphone, and wireless networking support. Note that the MacBook Air does *not* come with wired networking support or a CD or DVD drive.

MacBook Air Ports

The sides of the MacBook Air have a number of ports that enable you to connect a wide variety of devices.

Audio Out

You use the audio out port to play music or other audio through speakers or headphones.

USB

You use the MacBook Air's USB port to connect devices that support USB, including DVD drives, keyboards, mice, printers, cameras, external drives, and iPods.

MiniDisplay Port
Video Out

You use the MiniDisplay Port video out port to connect the MacBook Air to an additional display, such as a second monitor, a TV, or a video projector.

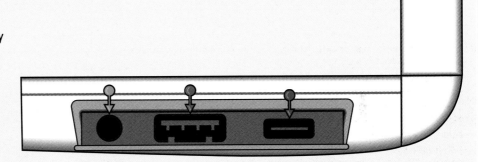

MacBook Air Accessories

MacBook Air SuperDrive

The MacBook Air does not come with a built-in CD or DVD drive, but you can attach the external MacBook Air SuperDrive to the USB port. The MacBook Air SuperDrive can read and write DVDs and CDs, and weighs just 0.71 pounds.

USB Ethernet Adapter

The MacBook Air does not offer a port for a wired network connection. If you need a faster network connection than the MacBook Air's built-in wireless networking, or if your local network offers only wired connections, you can attach the USB Network Adapter to the computer's USB port.

If you are thinking of purchasing a MacBook, or just want to know more about this Mac model, this section explains the MacBook's features and concepts.

MacBook Overview

The MacBook is a portable computer that combines the monitor and keyboard into a single unit. Instead of a mouse, the MacBook uses a trackpad where you move the pointer by sliding your finger along the pad.

MacBook Features

The MacBook uses an Intel Core 2 Duo processor; a 13.3-inch widescreen display (measured diagonally); 2GB of memory; a 250GB, 320GB, or 500GB hard drive; a built-in iSight camera and microphone; wired and wireless networking support; and a CD and DVD burner.

MacBook Features
Intel Core 2 Duo processor
iSight camera & microphone
13.3" widescreen display
2GB of memory
250GB to 500GB hard drive
CD & DVD burner
Wired & wireless network support

MacBook Ports

The sides of the MacBook have a number of ports that enable you to connect a wide variety of devices.

Network

You use the network port to connect the MacBook to a wired network.

Mini DisplayPort Video Out

You use the Mini DisplayPort video out port to connect the MacBook to an additional display, such as a second monitor, a TV, or a video projector.

USB

You use the MacBook's two USB ports to connect devices that support USB, including keyboards, mice, printers, cameras, external drives, and iPods.

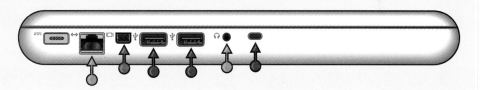

Audio In

You use the audio in port to bring speech or other audio into the MacBook using a microphone, musical instrument, or audio player.

Audio Out

You use the audio out port to play music or other audio through speakers or headphones.

Understanding What You Can Do with Your Mac

Are you ready to learn about what you can do with a Mac? In this chapter you find out about the wide variety of tasks you can perform with your Mac, including creating documents; playing music; organizing photos, contacts, and events; surfing the Web; and communicating with others.

You can use your Mac to create a wide variety of documents, including lists, letters, memos, budgets, forecasts, presentations, and Web pages.

Text Documents

You can use text editing software on your Mac to create simple documents such as lists, notes, instructions, and other items that do not require fonts, colors, or other types of formatting. On your Mac, you can use the TextEdit application to create plain text documents, and the Stickies application to create electronic sticky notes.

Word Processing Documents

You can use word processing software on your Mac to create letters, resumes, memos, reports, newsletters, brochures, business cards, menus, flyers, invitations, and certificates. Anything that you use to communicate on paper, you can create using your Mac. On your Mac, you can also use TextEdit to create formatted documents. Other examples include Microsoft Word for the Mac and Apple iWork Pages.

Spreadsheets

A *spreadsheet* is a software program that enables you to manipulate numbers and formulas to quickly create powerful mathematical, financial, and statistical models. Your Mac comes with a test drive version of the Numbers spreadsheet application, which is part of Apple's iWork suite. Another example is Microsoft Excel for the Mac.

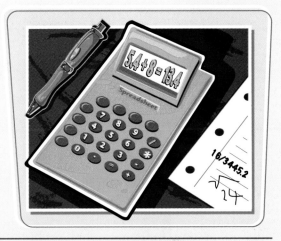

Presentations

A presentation program enables you to build professional-looking slides that you can use to convey your ideas to other people. Your Mac comes with a test drive version of the Keynote application, which is part of Apple's iWork suite. Another example is Microsoft PowerPoint for the Mac.

Web Pages

You can use Web page editing software on your Mac to create your own pages to publish to the Web. You can create a personal home page, a blog, or pages to support your business. On your Mac, you can use the iWeb application, which comes with the iLife suite, to create and publish entire Web sites.

Play and Record Music

Your Mac is a veritable music machine that you can use to organize and play your digital music collection. You can copy music from audio CDs, purchase music online, and even record new tunes.

iTunes

Your Mac comes with the iTunes application, which stores your library of digital music files. With iTunes you can play albums and songs, organize tunes into related playlists, download and edit track information, and organize your music to suit your style. You can also use iTunes to listen to Internet-based radio stations.

iTunes Store

You can use the iTunes application to connect directly to the online iTunes Store, where you can purchase individual songs, usually for 99 cents per song, or entire albums, usually for $9.99 per album. Your Mac downloads the purchased music to your iTunes Library, and you can listen to the music on your Mac or add the music to your iPod, iPad, or iPhone.

Import Music from a CD

You can add tracks from a music CD to the iTunes Library. This enables you to listen to an album without having to put the CD into your CD or DVD drive each time. In iTunes, the process of copying tracks from a CD to your Mac is called *importing* or *ripping*.

Record Music

Your Mac might come with an application called GarageBand that enables you to record your own tunes. You can attach an instrument such as a guitar or keyboard to your Mac and record your playing. You can also use GarageBand to add accompanying instruments such as drums, bass, piano, or another guitar.

Burn Music to a CD

You can copy, or *burn*, music files from your Mac onto a CD. Burning CDs is a great way to create customized CDs that you can listen to on the computer or in a portable device. You can burn music files using the iTunes application or using the GarageBand application.

Synchronize with an iPod, iPad, or iPhone

You can use the iTunes application to copy some or all of your music library to an iPod, iPad, or iPhone, which enables you to play your music while you are walking around or on another audio device that connects to the iPod, iPad, or iPhone. When you attach the iPod, iPad, or iPhone to your Mac using a USB cable, iTunes automatically synchronizes the device according to the settings you specify.

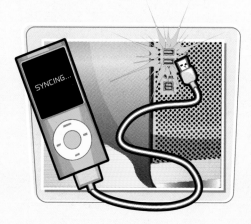

View and Organize Your Photos

Your Mac's high-quality display is perfect for displaying, organizing, and editing your digital photos. You can view photo slide shows, import images from a camera, take snapshots, and edit your photos.

View Photos

Your Mac gives you many ways to view your digital photos. If you have Mac OS X 10.5 (Leopard) or 10.6 (Snow Leopard), you can view photos within Finder using the Cover Flow view, or by selecting the photos and pressing Spacebar. You can also double-click a photo file to open it using the Preview application, or you can open a file using the iPhoto application, if it is installed. Also, both Preview and iPhoto enable you to run photo slide shows.

Organize Photos

If your Mac comes with iPhoto installed, you can use it to organize your Mac's collection of digital photos. For example, you can create albums of related photos, and you can create folders in which to store photos. You can also rename and rate photos, apply keywords to photos, flag important photos, and sort photos in various ways.

Import Photos to Your Mac

If you have a digital camera attached to your Mac, you can use either the Image Capture application or the iPhoto application to import some or all of the camera's images to your Mac.

Take Snapshots

If your Mac includes an iSight camera or has a digital video camera connected, you can use the Photo Booth application to take snapshots of whatever subject is currently displayed in the camera. You can also apply various effects to the photos.

Edit Photos

You can use the iPhoto application to edit your digital photos. You can rotate, crop, or straighten a photo; you can modify a photo's exposure, contrast, and sharpness; you can fix problems such as red eye and blemishes; and you can add special effects to a photo.

Play or Make a Movie or DVD

Your Mac's solid graphical underpinnings make it a great tool for playing digital movies and DVDs. You can also use your Mac to create your own digital movies and DVDs.

Play a DVD

If your Mac has a DVD drive, you can use the DVD Player application to play a DVD movie. You can either watch the movie in a window while you work on other things, or you can switch to full-screen mode and watch the movie using the entire screen. DVD Player has features that enable you to control the movie playback and volume.

Play a Video File

Your Mac comes with an application called QuickTime Player that can play digital video files. The basic version that comes with your Mac enables you to open video files and control the playback and volume. QuickTime Pro — which you can purchase for $29.99 — adds many extra features, including the ability to record movies and audio and to cut and paste scenes.

Play a Movie, TV Show, or Podcast

You most often use iTunes to play music, but you can also use it to play video files stored on your Mac, movies, and TV shows that you purchase from the iTunes Store, as well as podcasts that you download from the iTunes Store or subscribe to online.

Make a Movie

If your Mac has iLife installed, then it comes with an application called iMovie that enables you to make your own digital movies. You can import clips from a video camera or video file, add clips to the movie, and rearrange and trim those clips as needed. You can also add transitions between scenes, music and sound effects, titles, and more.

Make a DVD

You can use your Mac to create your own custom DVD discs. Using the iDVD application, which is part of the iLife suite, you can create a DVD project that includes video footage, photos, and audio effects. You can enhance the project with a custom menu, titles, and sophisticated background and text themes. When you are done, you can burn the project to a DVD disc.

Take Advantage of the Web

You can use your Mac to connect to the Internet and access the Web to look for information or news, buy and sell goods, socialize with others, and more.

Surf the Web

Your Mac comes with a browser application called Safari that you use to surf the Web. With Safari you can navigate Web pages, save favorite Web pages as bookmarks, and view multiple pages in a single window using tabs.

Search for Information

If you need information on a specific topic, free Web sites called *search engines* enable you to quickly search the Web for pages that have the information you require. You can search the Web either by going directly to a search engine site or by using the search feature built into Safari.

Read News

The Web is home to many sites that enable you to read the latest news. For example, many print sources have Web sites, some magazines exist only online, and there are more recent innovations such as blogs and RSS feeds. Some media sites require that you register to access the articles, but on most sites the registration is free.

Buy and Sell

E-commerce — the online buying and selling of goods and services — is a big part of the Web. You can use Web-based stores to purchase books, theater tickets, and even cars, which gives you the convenience of shopping at home, easily comparing prices and features, and having goods delivered to your door. Many sites also enable you to sell or auction your products or household items.

Socialize

The Web offers many opportunities to socialize, whether you are looking for a friend or a date, or you just want some good conversation. However, it is a good idea to observe some common-sense precautions. For example, arrange to meet new friends in public places, supervise all online socializing done by children, and do not give out personal information to strangers.

Take Advantage of MobileMe

For an extra charge, you can use your Mac to set up a Web-based MobileMe account that enables you to perform many activities online, including exchanging e-mail, maintaining contacts, tracking appointments, sharing photos, and storing files. You can also synchronize data between your Mac and your MobileMe account.

You can use your Mac to communicate with other people using online technologies such as e-mail and instant messaging.

Exchange E-Mail

E-mail is the Internet system that enables you to electronically exchange messages with other Internet users anywhere in the world. To use e-mail, you must have an e-mail account, which is usually supplied by your ISP. The account gives you an e-mail address to which others can send messages. You then set up that account in your Mac's Mail application.

Exchange E-Mail over the Web

You can also set up a Web-based e-mail account. Although you can do this using services such as Hotmail.com and Yahoo.com, many Mac users create MobileMe accounts, which include Web-based e-mail. A Web-based account is convenient because it enables you to send and receive messages from any computer that has access to the Internet.

Exchange Instant Messages

Instant messaging allows you to contact other people who are online, thus enabling you to have a real-time exchange of messages. Communicating in real time means that if you send a message to another person who is online, that message appears on the person's computer right away. If that person sends you a response, it appears on your computer right away. On your Mac, you use the iChat application to exchange instant messages.

Audio Chat

You can also use the iChat program to audio chat with another person. With an audio chat, you speak into a microphone and your voice is sent over the Internet to the other person who hears you through his or her computer's speakers. You also hear that person's voice through your own speakers.

Video Chat

You can also use the iChat program to video chat with someone. With a video chat, your image is captured by a video camera — such as the iSight camera built into many Macs — and a microphone captures your voice, and both the video and audio streams are sent over the Internet to the other person. You can also see and hear the other person on your Mac.

Organize Your Contacts and Events

You can use your Mac to help you organize your life. Specifically, your Mac comes with tools that enable you to manage your contacts and schedule your events.

Maintain Your Address Book

Your Mac comes with an application called Address Book that enables you to store information about your contacts. For each contact, you can store data such as the person's name, address, telephone number, e-mail address, birthday, and more.

Work with Contacts

You can use your Address Book items to perform many different contact-related tasks. For example, you can use Mail to send a message either to individual contacts or to a contact group, which is an Address Book item that contains multiple contacts. Also, you can use iCal to set up a meeting with a contact.

Schedule an Event

You can help organize your life by using your Mac to record your events on the date and time they occur. You do this using the iCal application, which uses an electronic calendar to store your events. You can even configure iCal to display a reminder before an event occurs.

Schedule an All-Day Event

If an event has no set time — for example, a birthday, anniversary, or multiple-day event such as a sales meeting or vacation — you can use iCal to set up the appointment as an all-day event.

Schedule a Repeating Event

If an event occurs regularly — for example, once a week or once every three months — you do not need to schedule every event by hand. Instead, you can use iCal to configure the activity as a repeating event, where you specify the repeat interval. iCal then creates all the future events automatically.

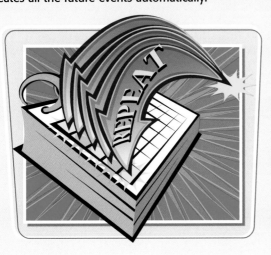

Synchronize with MobileMe

If you have a MobileMe account, you can synchronize your Mac's e-mail, contacts, and appointments so that they also appear in the MobileMe's Mail, Contacts, and Calendar applications. If you have a second Mac, you can use MobileMe to keep your e-mail, contacts, and appointments in sync on both Macs.

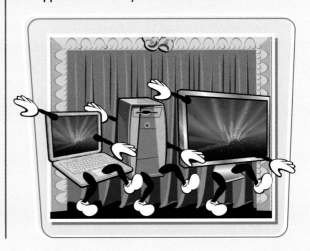

3

Connecting Devices to Your Mac

When you plug a device into your Mac, most of the time the device works right away. However, there are some devices that require a bit of extra effort on your part to get them connected and configured. This chapter takes you through a few such devices, including an external display, printer, fax, iPod, iPhone, iPad, Bluetooth device, and even another Mac.

Connect Your Mac to an External Display

You can connect your Mac to an external display such as a monitor or a TV. This is essential for machines such as the Mac mini and Mac Pro that do not come with a screen. However, you can also connect an iMac or portable Mac to a larger screen for more viewing area.

The Mac Connection

DVI Port

The Mac Pro, and older models of the Mac mini and MacBook Pro, use a regular DVI port to output video.

Mini DisplayPort

All of the latest Mac models come with a Mini DisplayPort. Apple offers separate adapters for connecting these ports to regular DVI displays.

DVI Port

Most computer monitors come with at least one DVI port, although the configuration (the number of holes) may not match what you have on your Mac. Therefore, the cable you use must have connectors that match the ports on both the Mac and the monitor.

VGA Port

Most computer monitors come with at least one VGA port. To use such a port with your Mac, you need a cable adapter that converts DVI or Mini DisplayPort to VGA.

Composite or S-Video Port

Most televisions come with either or both an S-Video port or a composite video port. To use such a port with your Mac, you need a cable adapter that converts DVI, Mini DisplayPort, or Micro DVI to either S-Video or composite video.

Cable Adapters

If you have a Mac that uses a Mini DisplayPort, you may need to purchase from Apple an adapter that enables you to connect your Mac to VGA or regular DVI display. You can also purchase from Apple an adapter that enables you to connect your Mac to a composite or S-Video display.

Connect a Printer

If you have a printer that you want to use to make hard copies of some of your documents, you must first connect the printer to your Mac.

① Connect the printer's USB cable to a free USB port on your Mac, and then turn on the printer.

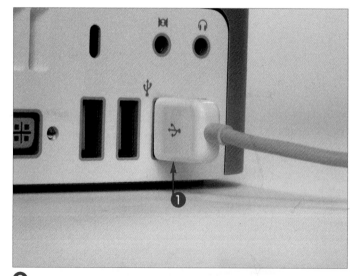

② Click the Apple icon ().

③ Click **System Preferences**.

Note: You can also click the System Preferences icon () in the Dock.

The System Preferences appear.

④ Click **Print & Fax**.

The Print & Fax preferences appear.

● If you see your printer in the Printers list, skip the rest of the steps in this section.

⑤ Click **Add** (＋).

The Add Printer dialog appears.

TIP

What do I do if my printer has a parallel port instead of a USB port?

Although almost all new printers come with USB ports, many older printers use a parallel (also called LPT) port instead. No Mac has a corresponding printer port, so you need to purchase a parallel-to-USB adapter cable, which has a parallel connector on one end and a USB connector on the other.

Fortunately, the vast majority of the time your Mac will recognize your printer immediately after you attach it to the USB port, so in most cases you will not need to use the extra steps in this section.

⑥ Click **Default**.

⑦ In the Printer Name list, click your printer.

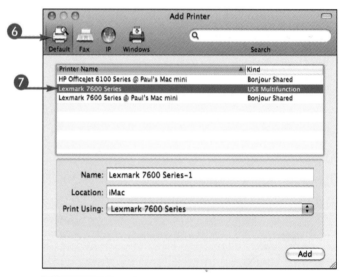

⑧ Use the Name text box to edit the printer name.

⑨ If the Print Using list shows the wrong printer, click 🛟 and then click the correct printer.

⑩ Click **Add**.

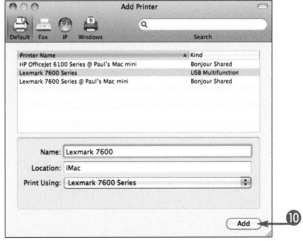

● OS X adds the printer to the
Printers list.

⑪ Click **Close** (●).

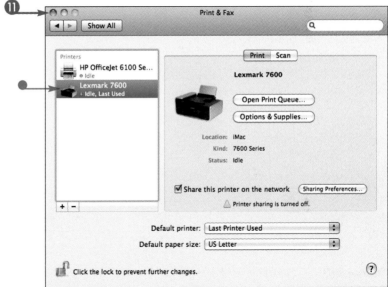

**What should I do if I do
not see my printer in the
Print Using list?**

First, insert the disc that came
with your printer and then run
the installation program. If that
does not work, follow Steps **1**
to **7** and then, in the Print Using list, click ▣
and then click **Other**. Click the printer disc,
locate and choose the printer driver, and then
click **Open**.

**What if I do not have a printer
disc?**

If you do not have a printer disc,
or if the disc does not contain
Mac drivers, visit the printer
manufacturer's Web site and
download the drivers you need. If
you cannot get drivers for the printer (many printer
manufacturers do not bother writing Mac drivers),
you may still be able to use the printer by choosing
Generic PostScript Printer in the Print Using list.

Connect a Fax Modem

If you want to send or receive faxes using your Mac, then you must connect an external fax modem, such as Apple's USB Modem.

Some older Macs came with an internal fax modem already installed, so you may not need to connect an external modem.

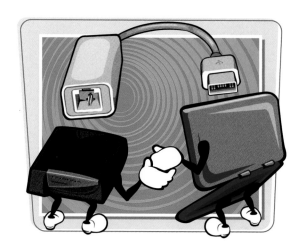

① Connect the fax modem to a free USB port on your Mac.

② Follow Steps **2** to **5** in the previous section to display the Add Printer dialog.

③ Click **Fax**.

Note: If you are using a version of OS X earlier than Leopard (10.5), click Default Browser instead.

④ In the Printer Name list, click your modem.

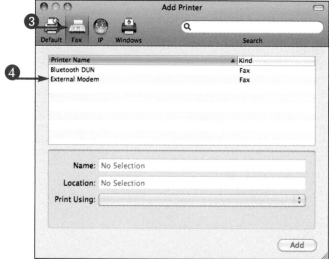

⑤ Use the Name text box to edit the modem name.

⑥ Click **Add**.

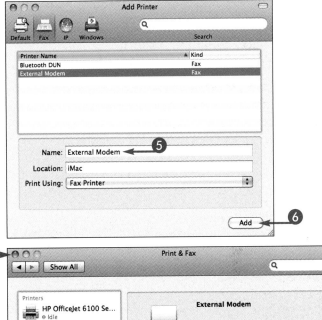

● OS X adds the modem to the Printers list.

⑦ Click 🔘.

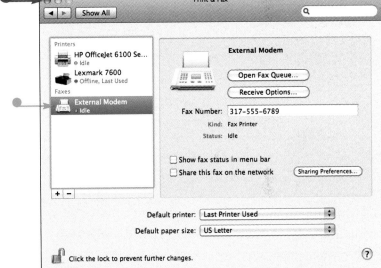

TIP

What do I do if my modem has a serial port instead of a USB port?

Although almost all new modems come with USB ports, many older modems use a serial port instead. No Mac has a corresponding serial port, so you need to purchase a serial-to-USB adapter or cable, which has a serial connector on one end and a USB connector on the other.

Connect an iPod

To synchronize some or all of your iTunes Library with your iPod, you need to connect the iPod to your Mac.

To connect an iPod you will need the USB cable that came with the iPod package.

Connect an iPod

Connect the iPod

1 Attach the USB connector to a free USB port on your Mac.

2 Attach the other end of the USB cable to the iPod's port.

Your Mac launches iTunes and automatically begins synchronizing the iPod.

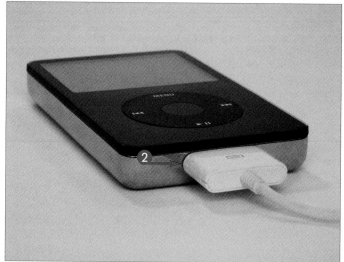

Disconnect the iPod

① In iTunes, click the eject button (⏏) beside your iPod's name.

iTunes begins releasing the iPod.

Note: *See the following Tip to learn when it is safe to disconnect the cable from the iPod.*

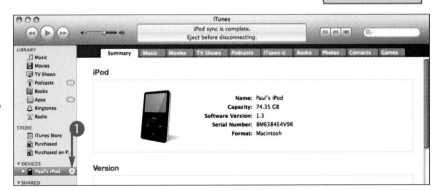

② Pinch the sides of the connector and then pull the connector away from the iPod.

③ Disconnect the cable from the Mac's USB port.

Note: *If your Mac has two or more free USB ports and you synchronize your iPod frequently, consider leaving the cable plugged into a USB port for easier iPod connections in the future.*

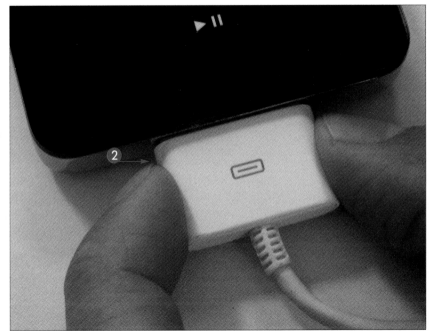

TIP

Do I always have to eject my iPod before disconnecting it?

No, not always. You must first eject the iPod if the iPod screen says "Do not disconnect," "Eject Before Disconnecting," or "Sync in Progress." You can safely disconnect the cable from your iPod if the iPod screen says "OK to disconnect," "Charging," "Charged," or you see the iPod main menu screen.

Connect an iPhone

To synchronize some or all of your iTunes Library, Address Book contacts, iCal appointments, Safari bookmarks, and e-mail account settings with your iPhone, you need to connect the iPhone to your Mac.

To connect an iPhone you will need the USB cable that came with the iPhone package. You can also connect an iPhone using an optional dock.

Connect an iPhone

Connect the iPhone Directly

1 Attach the USB connector to a free USB port on your Mac.

2 Attach the other end of the USB cable to the iPhone's port.

Your Mac launches iTunes and automatically begins synchronizing the iPhone.

Connect the iPhone Using the Dock

① Attach the USB connector to a free USB port on your Mac.

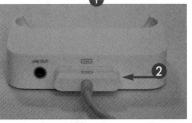

② Attach the other end of the USB cable to the iPhone dock's port.

③ Insert the iPhone into the dock.

Your Mac launches iTunes and automatically begins synchronizing the iPhone.

TIP

How do I disconnect the iPhone?
First, make sure that the iPhone is not currently synchronizing, in which case it shows "Sync in Progress" on the screen. When the screen says "iPhone sync is complete," you can disconnect the iPhone. In iTunes, click the eject button (⏏) beside your iPhone's name. If you are using the USB cable, pinch the sides of the iPhone connector and then pull the connector away from the iPhone. If you are using the dock, lift the iPhone out of the dock.

To synchronize some or all of your iTunes Library, Address Book contacts, iCal appointments, Safari bookmarks, and e-mail account settings with your iPad, you need to connect the iPad to your Mac.

To connect an iPad you will need the USB cable that came with the iPad package. You can also connect an iPad using an optional dock.

Connect the iPad Directly

1 Attach the USB connector to a free USB port on your Mac.

2 Attach the other end of the USB cable to the iPad's port.

Your Mac launches iTunes and automatically begins synchronizing the iPad.

Connect the iPad Using the Dock

1 Attach the USB connector to a free USB port on your Mac.

2 Attach the other end of the USB cable to the iPad dock's port.

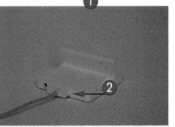

3 Insert the iPad into the dock.

Your Mac launches iTunes and automatically begins synchronizing the iPad.

 TIP

How do I disconnect the iPad?
First, make sure that the iPad is not currently synchronizing, in which case it shows "Sync in Progress" on the screen. When the screen says "iPad sync is complete," you can disconnect the iPad. In iTunes, click the eject button (⏏) beside your iPad's name. If you are using the USB cable, pinch the sides of the iPad connector and then pull the connector away from the iPad. If you are using the dock, lift the iPad out of the dock.

Connect a Bluetooth Device

You can make wireless connections to devices such as mice, keyboards, headsets, and cell phones by using the Bluetooth networking technology.

For Bluetooth connections to work, your Mac must support Bluetooth (all newer Macs do) and your device must be Bluetooth-enabled.

Connect a Generic Bluetooth Device

① Perform whatever steps are necessary to make your Bluetooth device discoverable. (See the first Tip on the following page.)

Note: *For example, if you are connecting a Bluetooth mouse, the device often has a separate switch or button that makes the mouse discoverable, so you need to turn on that switch or press that button.*

② Click the Bluetooth status icon (⚹).

③ Click **Set Up Bluetooth Device**.

The Bluetooth Setup Assistant appears.

The Bluetooth Setup Assistant begins searching for Bluetooth devices within range.

● The list of discovered devices appears here.

④ Click the Bluetooth device you want to connect.

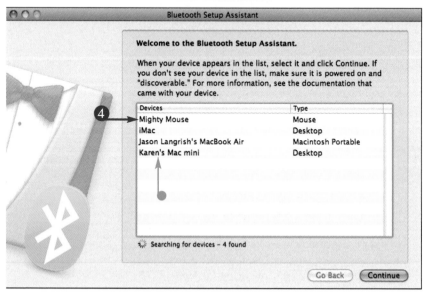

5 Click **Continue**.

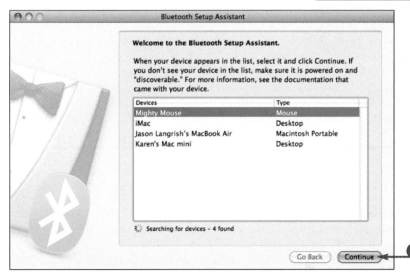

6 Perform the steps required to pair your Mac and your device.

Note: See the next two pages for the pairing instructions for a keyboard, headset, and cell phone. A Bluetooth mouse does not require any extra pairing steps.

Your Mac connects with the device.

7 Click **Quit**.

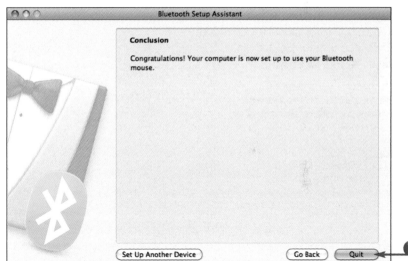

What does it mean to make a device "discoverable"?

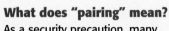

This means that you configure the device to broadcast that it is available for a Bluetooth connection. Controlling the broadcast is important because you usually want to use a Bluetooth device such as a mouse or keyboard with only a single computer. By controlling when the device is discoverable, you ensure that it works only with the computer you want it to.

What does "pairing" mean?

As a security precaution, many Bluetooth devices do not connect automatically to other devices. This makes sense because otherwise it means a stranger with a Bluetooth device could connect to your cell phone or even your Mac. To prevent this, most Bluetooth devices require you to enter a passcode before the connection is made. This is known as *pairing* the two devices.

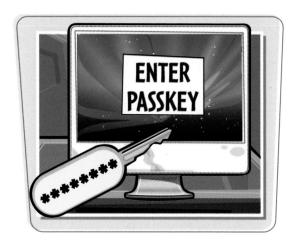

In most cases, pairing is accomplished by your Mac generating an 8-digit *passcode* that you must then type into the Bluetooth device (assuming that it has some kind of keypad). In other cases, the device comes with a default passkey that you must enter into your Mac to set up the pairing.

Connect a Bluetooth Device *(continued)*

Connect a Bluetooth Keyboard

1 Turn on the keyboard, if required.

2 Turn on the switch or press the button that makes the keyboard discoverable, if required.

3 Follow Steps **1** to **5** from earlier in this section.

Note: *When the Bluetooth Setup Assistant displays the list of devices, click your keyboard in the list.*

The Bluetooth Setup Assistant displays a passkey.

4 Use the Bluetooth keyboard to type the displayed passkey.

Connect a Bluetooth Headset

1 Turn on the headset.

2 Turn on the switch that makes the headset discoverable.

3 Follow Steps **1** to **3** from earlier in this section.

The Bluetooth Setup Assistant displays a list of devices within range.

4 Click the Bluetooth headset.

5 Click **Continue**.

Your Mac connects with the headset.

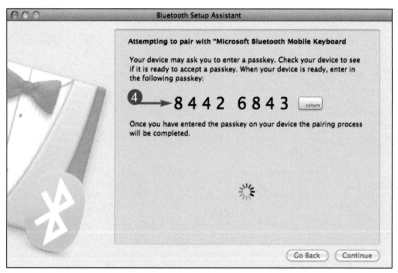

Connect a Bluetooth Cell Phone

① Turn on the cell phone.

② Make the cell phone discoverable.

③ Follow Steps **1** to **3** from earlier in this section.

The Bluetooth Setup Assistant displays a list of devices within range.

④ Click the Bluetooth cell phone.

⑤ Click **Continue**.

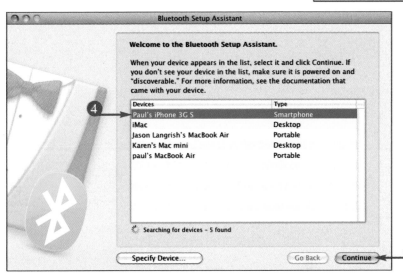

The Bluetooth Setup Assistant displays a passkey.

⑥ Use the Bluetooth phone's keypad to type the displayed passkey.

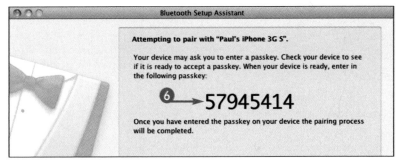

How do I remove a Bluetooth device?
Follow these steps:

① Click ▣ in the menu bar.

② Click **Open Bluetooth Preferences**.

You can also click ▣, click **System Preferences**, and then click **Bluetooth**.

The Bluetooth preferences appear.

③ Click the device you want to remove.

④ Click **Remove** (−).

Your Mac asks you to confirm.

⑤ Click **Remove**.

Your Mac removes the device.

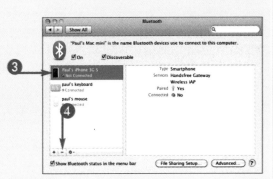

Connect Your Mac to Another Mac

You can share data such as documents, bookmarks, and downloads between two Macs by connecting those Macs using a network cable or a FireWire cable.

This task assumes that you do not have a local area network set up, so you need to connect the two Macs directly. In either case, you must enable file sharing to share data between the Macs.

Connect Your Mac to Another Mac

Connect Using a Network Cable

① Attach one of the network cable's connectors to the network port on one of the Macs.

② Attach the other network cable connector to the network port on the other Mac.

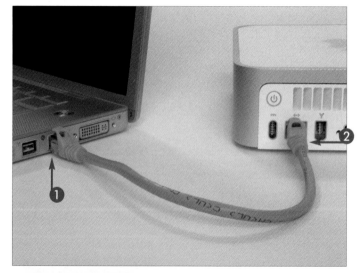

Connect Using a FireWire Cable

① Attach one of the FireWire cable's connectors to the FireWire port on one of the Macs.

② Attach the other FireWire cable connector to the FireWire port on the other Mac.

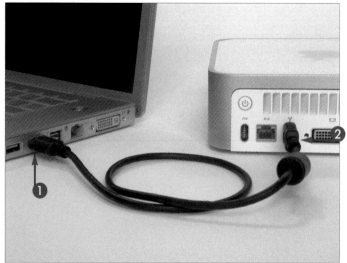

Enable File Sharing

① Click .

② Click **System Preferences**.

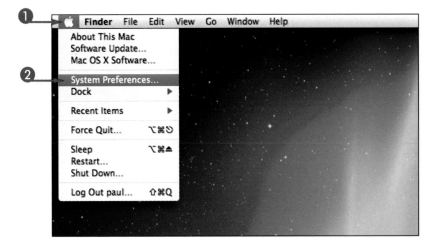

The System Preferences window appears.

③ Click **Sharing**.

Can I use a regular network cable?

Yes, for many Macs. However, some older Macs require a special crossover cable. You must use such a cable if you want to connect any of the following Macs:

eMac	iMac (Flat Panel)	Power Mac G4 Cube
iBook	iMac (Slot Loading)	Power Macintosh G3 (Blue and White)
iBook (FireWire)	iMac (Summer 2000)	
iMac	iMac (Summer 2001)	PowerBook (FireWire)
iMac (17-inch Flat Panel)	Power Mac G4 (AGP Graphics)	PowerBook G3 Series (Bronze Keyboard)
iMac (Early 2001)	Power Mac G4 (PCI Graphics)	

continued

You must enable file sharing on both Macs. Once you have done that, you can see the files shared on the other Mac by accessing Finder's Network folder.

The Sharing preferences appear.

④ Click **File Sharing** (☐ changes to ☑).

Note: *See the Tip on the following page to learn how to share other folders on your Mac.*

⑤ Click 🖼.

View the Other Mac's Files

① Click 🖼.

② Click the icon for the other Mac.

Note: *If you do not see an icon for the other Mac, click **Go** and then click **Network**, or press* Shift + ⌘ + K.

● Your Mac connects to the other Mac using the Guest account.

③ Click **Connect As**.

Your Mac prompts you to log in to the other Mac.

④ Use the Name text box to type the user name of an account on the other Mac.

⑤ Use the Password text box to type the password of an account on the other Mac.

⑥ Click **Connect**.

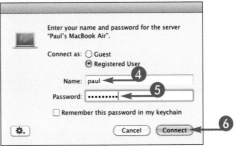

Your Mac logs in to the other Mac.

● You see the folder associated with the user account that you used to log in to the other Mac.

⑦ Click a folder to see and work with its contents.

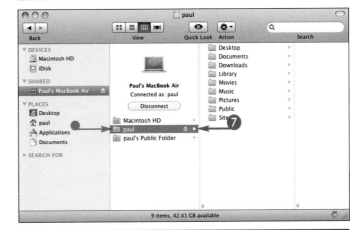

TIP

How do I share other folders?

Follow these steps to share another folder:

① Click .

② Click **System Preferences**.

The System Preferences window appears.

③ Click **Sharing**.

④ Click **File Sharing**.

⑤ Under the Shared Folders list, click ➕.

⑥ Click the folder you want to share.

⑦ Click **Add**.

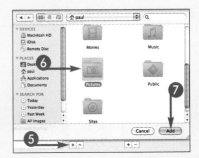

4

Learning Mac Basics

The OS X operating system is installed on all new Macintosh computers. You can use OS X to start programs, manage files, connect to the Internet, and perform computer maintenance, and so it is important to have a basic understanding of how OS X works.

Before you can begin to understand how the OS X operating system works, you should become familiar with the basic screen elements.

Menu Bar

The menu bar contains the pull-down menus for OS X and most OS X software.

Desktop

This is the OS X work area. It is where you work with your programs and documents.

Mouse Pointer

When you move your mouse, the pointer ‸ moves along with it.

Desktop Icon

An icon on the desktop represents a program or an OS X feature on your computer. This can be a disk drive, a CD or DVD, an iPod, or a document.

Dock

The Dock contains several icons, each of which gives you quick access to some commonly used programs.

The Dock gives you one-click access to programs, folders, and documents.

Finder

Use Finder to work with the files on your computer.

Dashboard

Use Dashboard to access several cool and handy mini applications called *widgets*.

Mail

Use Mail to send and receive e-mail messages.

Safari

Use Safari to browse the World Wide Web on the Internet.

iChat

Use iChat to converse with other people in real time by sending each other messages via text, audio, or video.

Address Book

Use the Address Book to store people's names, addresses, phone numbers, and other contact information.

iCal

Use iCal to keep track of your schedule.

Preview

Use Preview to view images.

iTunes

Use iTunes to play music files and audio CDs and to add music to your iPod, iPad, or iPhone.

iPhoto

Use iPhoto to import and edit digital photos and other images.

iMovie

Use iMovie to import and edit digital video movies.

iDVD

Use iDVD to burn images or video to a DVD disc.

GarageBand

Use GarageBand to create songs, podcasts, and other audio files.

iWeb

Use iWeb to create Web pages.

Photo Booth

Use Photo Booth to take pictures or videos using a camera attached to your Mac.

Time Machine

Use Time Machine to access backups of your files.

System Preferences

Use System Preferences to customize your Mac.

Applications

Use Applications to access your Mac's programs.

Documents

Use Documents to display the contents of your Documents folder.

Downloads

Use Downloads to display the contents of your Downloads folder.

Trash

Use the Trash to delete files.

Start a Program

To work with any program, you must first tell OS X which program you want to run. OS X then launches the program and displays it on the desktop.

① Click the **Finder** icon (⬜).

If the program that you want to start has an icon in the Dock, you can click the icon to start the program and skip the rest of these steps.

The Finder window appears.

② Click **Applications**.

Note: You can also navigate to Applications in any Finder window by pressing **Shift** + **⌘** + **A**.

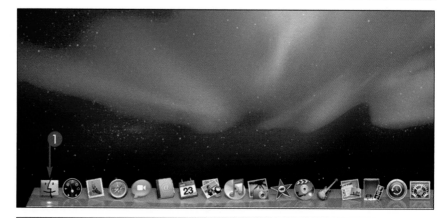

The Applications window appears.

③ Double-click the icon of the program that you want to start.

Note: *If you see a folder icon (▢), it means that the program resides in its own folder, a storage area on the computer. Double-click ▢ to open the folder and then double-click the program icon.*

● The program appears on the desktop.

● OS X adds a button for the program to the Dock and displays a blue smudge beneath the program icon to remind you that the program is running.

● The menu bar displays the menus associated with the program.

TIPS

How do I add an icon to the Dock for a program I use frequently?

First, start the program as described in Steps **1** to **3**. Control +click or right-click the program's Dock icon and then click **Keep In Dock**.

How do I shut down a running program?

The easiest way is to Control +click or right-click the program's Dock icon and then click **Quit**. Alternatively, you can press ⌘ + Q.

Switch Between Programs

With OS X, if you are *multitasking* — running two or more programs at once — you can easily switch from one program to another.

Switch Between Programs

① Click the Dock icon of the program to which you want to switch.

● OS X brings the program's windows to the foreground.

● The menu bar displays the menus associated with the program.

Note: *To switch between windows from the keyboard, press and hold* ⌘ *and repeatedly press* Tab *until the window that you want is highlighted in the list of running programs. Release* ⌘ *to switch to the window.*

You work with a program by accessing the various features in the program window.

Close Button

Click the **Close** button (🔘) to remove the program window from the desktop, usually without exiting the program.

Minimize Button

Click the **Minimize** button (🔘) to remove the window from the desktop and display an icon for the currently open document in the right side of the Dock. The window is still open, but not active.

Zoom Button

Click the Zoom button (🔘) to enlarge the window so it can display as much of its content as possible.

Title Bar

The title bar displays the name of the program. In some programs, the title bar also displays the name of the open document. To move the window, click and drag the title bar.

Toolbar

The toolbar contains buttons that offer easy access to common program commands and features.

Show/Hide Toolbar

Click 🔘 to toggle the toolbar on and off.

Status Bar

The status bar displays information about the current state of the program or document.

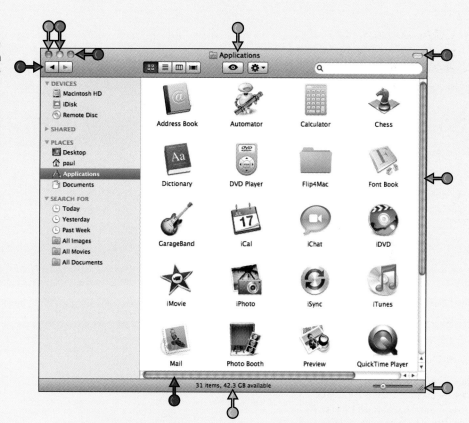

Vertical Scrollbar

Use the vertical scrollbar to navigate up and down in a document. Click **Scroll Up** (▲) to navigate up; click **Scroll Down** (▼) to navigate down.

Horizontal Scrollbar

Use the horizontal scrollbar to navigate left and right in a document. Click **Scroll Left** (◀) to navigate left; click **Scroll Right** (▶) to navigate right.

Resize Button

Click and drag 🔲 in the lower right corner of the window to make the window larger or smaller.

Select a Command from a Pull-Down Menu

When you are working in a program, you can use the menu bar to access the program's commands and features.

The items in a menu are either commands that execute an action in the program, or features that you can turn on and off.

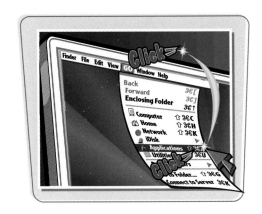

Select a Command from a Pull-Down Menu

Execute Commands

1 Click the name of the menu that you want to display.

● The program displays the menu.

2 Click the command that you want to execute.

The program executes the command.

If your command appears in a submenu, first click the command that opens the submenu, and then click the command that you want to run.

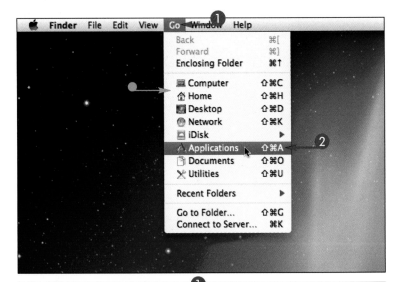

Turn Features On and Off

1 Click the name of the menu that you want to display.

● The program displays the menu.

2 Click the menu item.

You may have to click for a submenu if your command is not on the main menu.

The program turns the feature either on with a check mark (☑) or off (no check mark appears).

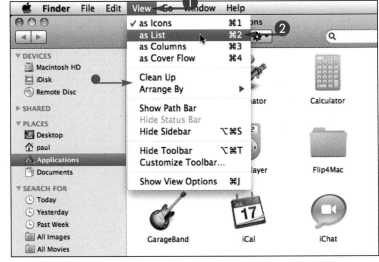

Select a Command Using a Toolbar

You can access commands faster using the toolbar. Most programs come with a toolbar, which is a collection of buttons that gives you one-click access to the program's most common features.

Select a Command Using a Toolbar

Turn Features On and Off

1 Click the toolbar button that represents the feature you want to turn on.

● The program turns the feature on and indicates this state by highlighting the toolbar button.

● When a feature is turned off, the program does not highlight the button.

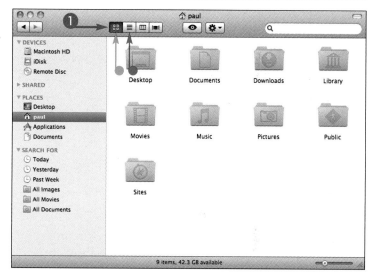

Execute Commands

1 Click the toolbar button that represents the command that you want.

2 If the button displays a menu, click the command on the menu.

● The program executes the command.

Select Options with Dialog Controls

Dialogs appear when a program needs you to provide information. For example, when you select the File menu's Print command to print a document, you use the Print dialog to specify the number of copies that you want to print. You provide that and other information by accessing various types of dialog controls.

Command Button

Clicking a command button executes the command written on the button face. For example, you can click **OK** to apply settings that you have chosen in a dialog, or you can click **Cancel** to close the dialog without changing the settings.

Text Box

A text box enables you to enter typed text. Use the `Del` key to delete any existing characters, and then type your text.

List Box

A list box displays a list of choices from which you can select the item you want. Use the vertical scrollbar to bring the item you want into view, and then click the item to select it.

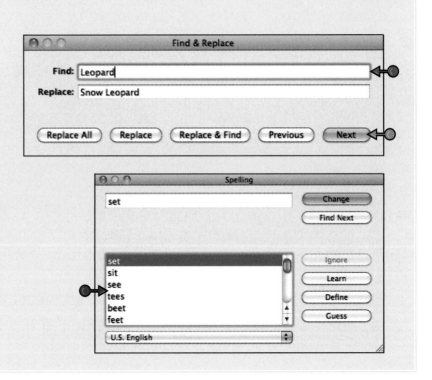

Pop-Up Menu

A pop-up menu displays a list of choices from which you select the item you want. Click ⊞ to pop up the menu, and then click the item that you want to select.

Check Box

Clicking a check box toggles a program feature on and off. If you are turning on a feature, the check box changes from ☐ to ☑; if you are turning off the feature, the check box changes from ☑ to ☐.

Radio Button

Clicking a radio button turns on a program feature. Only one radio button in a group can be turned on at a time. When you click a radio button, it changes from ◯ to ◉.

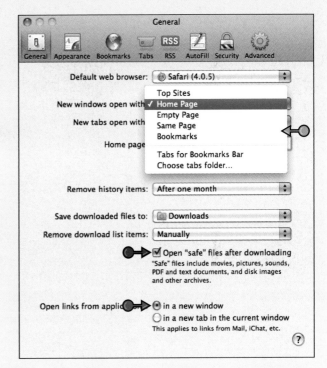

Save a Document

After you create a document and make changes to it, you can save the document to preserve your work.

When you work on a document, OS X stores the changes in your computer's memory, which is erased each time you shut down your computer. Saving the document preserves your changes on your computer's hard drive.

Save a Document

① Click **File**.

② Click **Save**.

In most programs, you can also press ⌘ + Ⓢ.

If you have saved the document previously, your changes are now preserved, and you do not need to follow the rest of the steps in this section.

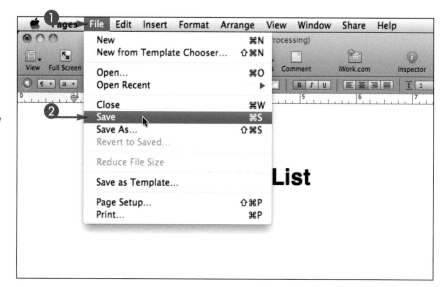

● If this is a new document that you have never saved before, the Save dialog appears.

③ Click in the **Save As** text box and type the name that you want to use for the document.

● To select a different folder in which to store the file, you can click ⬦ in the Where pop-up menu and then click the location that you prefer.

④ Click **Save**.

The program saves the file.

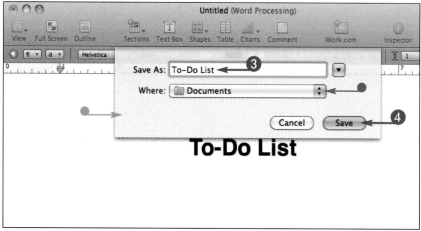

Open a Document

To work with a document that you have saved in the past, you can open it in the program that you used to create it.

Open a Document

① Start the program that you want to work with.

② Click **File**.

③ Click **Open**.

In most programs, you can also press ⌘ + O.

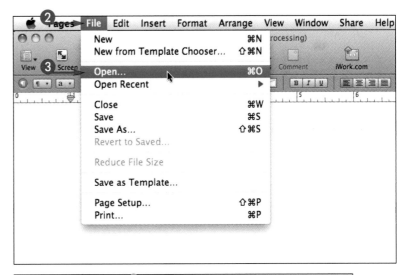

● The Open dialog appears.

● To select a different folder from which to open the file, you can click ▣ in the list and then click the location that you prefer.

④ Click the document.

⑤ Click **Open**.

The document appears in the program window.

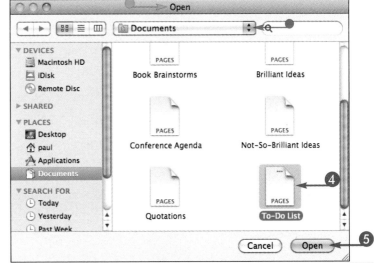

When you need a hard copy of your document, either for your files or to distribute to someone else, you can send the document to your printer.

① Turn on your printer.

② Open the document that you want to print.

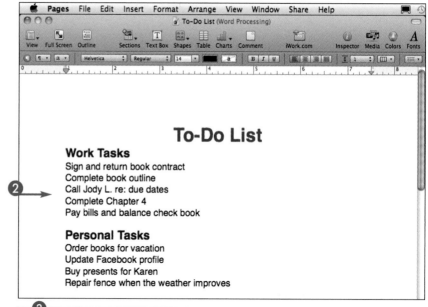

③ Click **File**.

④ Click **Print**.

In many programs, you can also select the Print command by pressing ⌘ + P.

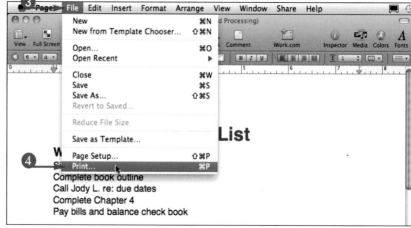

The Print dialog appears.

The layout of the Print dialog varies from program to program. The version shown here is a typical example.

⑤ If you have more than one printer, click ▦ the Printer pop-up menu to select the printer that you want to use.

● To print more than one copy, click ▾ to expand the dialog, then use the Copies text box to type the number of copies to print.

⑥ Click **Print**.

● OS X prints the document. The printer icon appears in the Dock while the document prints.

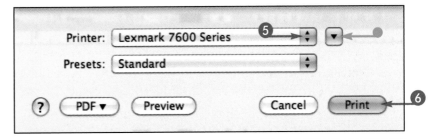

Can I preview my document before I print it?

Yes. It is a good idea to preview the document before printing it to ensure that the document layout looks the way you want. To preview the document, follow Steps **1** to **4** in this section to display the Print dialog. Click **Preview** to display the document in the Preview window. When you are done, click **Preview** and then click **Quit Preview**.

Edit Document Text

When you work with a character-based file, such as a text or word-processing document or an e-mail message, you need to know the basic techniques for editing, selecting, copying, and moving text.

Delete Characters

1 In a text document, click immediately to the right of the last character that you want to delete.

● The cursor appears after the character.

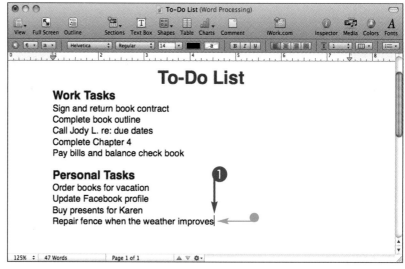

2 Press Del until you have deleted all the characters you want.

If you make a mistake, immediately click **Edit**, and then click **Undo**. You can also press ⌘+Z.

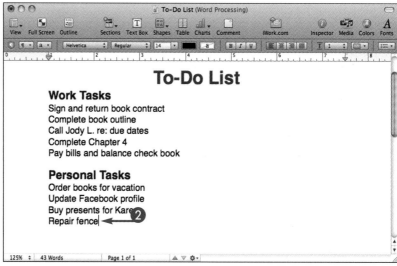

Select Text for Editing

1 Click and drag across the text that you want to select.

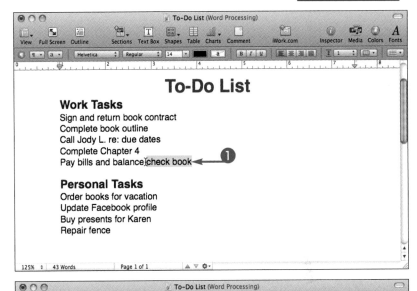

2 Release the mouse button.

● The program highlights the selected text.

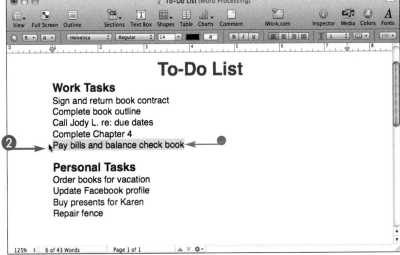

TIP

Are there any shortcut methods for selecting text?

Yes, most OS X programs have shortcuts you can use. Here are the most useful ones:

- Double-click a word to select it.
- Triple-click inside a paragraph to select it.
- In Microsoft Word for the Mac, ⌘-click to select a sentence.
- Press ⌘ + A to select the entire document.

continued

After you select text, you can copy or move it to another location in your document.

Copy Text

1. Select the text that you want to copy.

2. Click **Edit**.

3. Click **Copy**.

   In most programs, you can also press ⌘ + C.

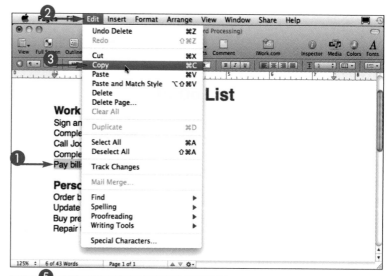

4. Click inside the document at the position where you want the copy of the text to appear.

   The cursor appears in the position where you clicked.

5. Click **Edit**.

6. Click **Paste**.

   In most programs, you can also press ⌘ + V.

● The program inserts a copy of the selected text at the cursor position.

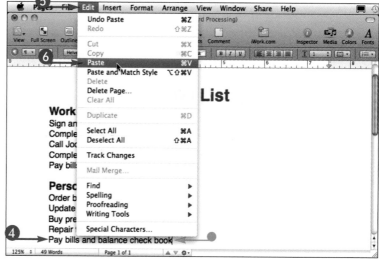

Move Text

1 Select the text that you want to move.

2 Click **Edit**.

3 Click **Cut**.

In most programs, you can also press ⌘ + X.

The program removes the text from the document.

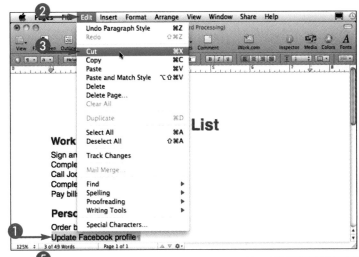

4 Click inside the document at the position where you want to move the text.

The cursor appears at the position where you clicked.

5 Click **Edit**.

6 Click **Paste**.

In most programs, you can also press ⌘ + V.

● The program inserts the text at the cursor position.

How do I move and copy text with my mouse?

First, select the text that you want to move or copy. To move the selected text, position the mouse pointer over the selection and then click and drag the text to the new position within the document.

To copy the selected text, position the mouse pointer over the selection, press and hold the Option key, and then click and drag the text to the new position within the document.

You can make an exact copy of a file. This is useful when you want to make a backup of an important file, if you want to create a new file that is similar to the existing file, or if you want to send the copy on a disk to another person.

You can copy either a single file or multiple files. You can also use this technique to copy a folder.

Copy a File

1. Locate the file that you want to copy.

2. Open the folder to which you want to copy the file.

   To open a second folder window, click **File** and then click **New Finder Window**, or press ⌘+N.

3. Press and hold the **Option** key, and then click and drag the file.

● The ▢ changes to ▸.

4. Drop the file inside the destination folder.

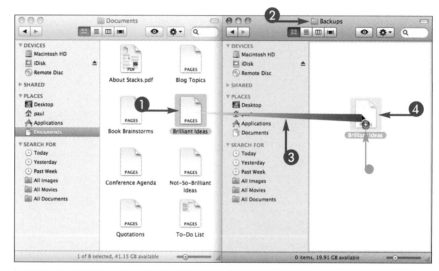

● The original file remains in its folder.

● A copy of the original file appears in the destination folder.

   You can also make a copy of a file in the same folder, which is useful if you want to make major changes to the file and you would like to preserve a copy of the original. Click the file, click **File**, and then click **Duplicate**, or press ⌘+D. OS X creates a copy with the word "copy" added to the filename.

Move a File

When you need to store a file in a new location, the easiest way is to move the file from its current folder to another folder on your computer.

You can use this technique to move a single file, multiple files, and even a folder.

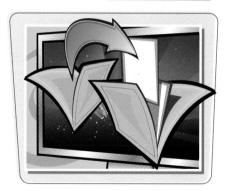

Move a File

1 Locate the file that you want to move.

2 Open the folder to which you want to move the file.

To create a new destination folder in the current folder, click **File** and then click **New Folder**, or press Shift + ⌘ + N.

3 Click and drag the file.

4 Drop the file inside the destination folder.

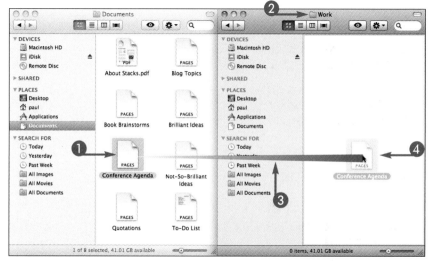

● The file disappears from its original folder.

● The file moves to the destination folder.

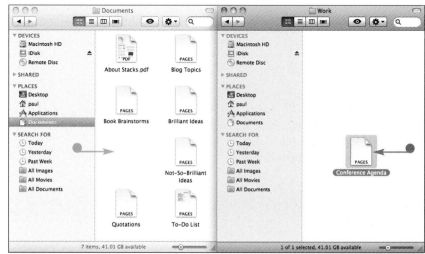

Rename a File

You can change the name of a file, which is useful if the current filename does not accurately describe the contents of the file. By giving your document a descriptive name, you make it easier to find the file later.

You should only rename those documents that you have created or that have been given to you by someone else. Do not rename any of the OS X system files or any files associated with your programs, or your computer may behave erratically, or even crash.

Rename a File

1 Open the folder containing the file that you want to rename.

2 Click the file.

3 Press Return.

● A text box appears around the filename.

You can also rename any folders that you have created.

4 Edit the existing name or type a new name that you want to use for the file.

If you decide that you do not want to rename the file after all, you can press Esc to cancel the operation.

5 Press Return or click an empty section of the folder.

● The new name appears under the file icon.

Delete a File

When you no longer need a file, you can delete it. This helps to prevent your hard drive from becoming cluttered with unnecessary files.

You should ensure that you delete only those documents that you have created or that have been given to you by someone else. Do not delete any of the OS X system files or any files associated with your programs, or your computer may behave erratically, or even crash.

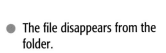

Delete a File

① Locate the file that you want to delete.

② Click and drag the file and drop it on the Trash icon in the Dock.

● The file disappears from the folder.

If you delete a file accidentally, you can restore it. Click the Dock's Trash icon to open the Trash window, Control +click or right-click the file, and then click **Put Back**.

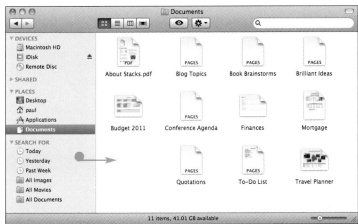

Playing and Organizing Music

Using iTunes, you can create a library of music and use that library to play songs, albums, and collections of songs called playlists; tune in to an Internet radio station; and subscribe to podcasts. You can also use iTunes to listen to music CDs, manage music on an iPod, and purchase music from the online iTunes Store.

Open and Close iTunes

Your Mac includes iTunes to enable you to play back and manage various types of audio files. To begin using the program, you must first learn how to find and open the iTunes window. When you finish using the program, you can close the iTunes window to free up computer processing power.

Open iTunes

1 Click **Finder** (image) in the Dock.

2 Click **Applications**.

3 Double-click **iTunes**.

The iTunes window appears.

84

Close iTunes

1. Click **iTunes**.

2. Click **Quit iTunes**.

TIPS

Are there faster methods I can use to open and close iTunes?

The fastest way to start iTunes is to click the iTunes icon ([icon]) in the Dock. If you have used iTunes recently, another reasonably fast method is to click the Apple icon ([icon]), click **Recent Items**, and then click **iTunes**. Probably the fastest method you can use to quit iTunes is to click **Close** ([icon]). Alternatively, Control +click or right-click the iTunes icon ([icon]) and then click **Quit**. Finally, if your hands are closer to the keyboard than to the mouse, you can quit iTunes by pressing [icon]+[icon].

Can I use iTunes for more than music?

Yes, iTunes is a versatile application that supports a number of different media, including movies, TV shows, podcasts, and Internet radio broadcasts. iTunes is also integrated with the iTunes Store, which you can use to download music, movies, and other media, usually for a small fee. You can also use iTunes to synchronize media with an iPod, iPad, or iPhone.

Understanding the iTunes Library

Most of your iTunes time will be spent in the Library, so you need to understand what you are working with.

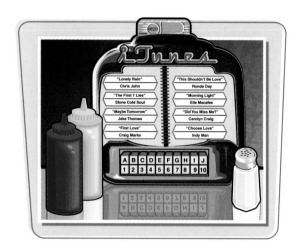

The iTunes Library

The iTunes Library is where your Mac stores the files that you can play and work with in the iTunes application. The iTunes Library includes not only the audio features discussed in this chapter, but also movies, TV shows, games, and more. Each section of the Library shows you the contents of that section and the details for each item, such as the name of each song and the artist who recorded it.

Audio in the Library

Although iTunes has some video components, its focus is on audio features, so most of the Library sections are audio-related. These sections include Music, Podcasts, Books, and Radio. Your iTunes Library also includes a Ringtones section for storing ringtones that you can add to a phone, such as an iPhone.

Familiarizing yourself with the various elements of the iTunes window is a good idea so that you can easily navigate and activate elements when you are ready to play audio files, podcasts, or listen to Internet radio.

Playback Controls

These buttons control media playback and enable you to adjust the volume.

Status Area

This area displays information about the item that is currently playing or the action that iTunes is currently performing.

View Options

You use these buttons to control how the contents of the current category appear. Click **List** (▤) to view the contents as a list; click **Grid** (▦) to view the contents as thumbnail icons; click **Cover Flow** (▥) to view the contents as a scrolling list of thumbnails.

Contents

The contents of the current iTunes Library source appear here.

Sources

This area displays the iTunes Library sources that you can view. Sources can include media categories, connected devices, and playlists.

Genius Sidebar

This area displays a list of songs, albums, or other iTunes Store content similar to the current item in the Library.

Status Bar

This area displays information about the contents of the current source or the selected media, such as the total items, size, and playing time.

You use the Music category of the iTunes Library to play a song that is stored on your computer. If you need to leave the room or take a call, you can also pause the currently playing song.

1 Click **Music**.

2 Click the view you prefer to use, such as the Grid view shown here.

Note: If you choose the List view, skip to Step 4.

3 Double-click the album that contains the song you want to play.

● If you want to play the entire album, click **Play Album**.

4 Click the song you want to play.

5 Click the **Play** button (▶).

iTunes begins playing the song.

● Information about the song playback appears here.

● iTunes displays a speaker icon () beside the currently playing song.

● If you need to stop the song temporarily, click the **Pause** button (▢).

Note: *You can also pause and restart a song by pressing the* Spacebar.

● You can use the Volume slider to adjust the volume (see the Tip below).

Note: *See the "Play a Music CD" section to learn more about the playback buttons.*

 TIP

How do I adjust the volume?

To turn the volume up or down, click and drag the **Volume** slider to the left (to reduce the volume) or to the right (to increase the volume). You can also press ⌘+⬇ to reduce the volume, or ⌘+⬆ to increase the volume.

To mute the volume, either drag the Volume slider all the way to the left, or press Option+⌘+⬇. To restore the volume, adjust the Volume slider or press Option+⌘+⬇.

You can play your favorite music CDs in iTunes. The CD appears in the Devices section, which displays the individual tracks on the CD. During playback, you can skip tracks and pause and resume play.

To play a music CD, your Mac must have a CD or DVD drive.

Play a CD

1 Insert a music CD into your Mac's CD or DVD drive.

● The music CD appears in iTune's Devices category.

  iTunes asks if you want to import the CD.

2 Click **No**.

Note: *To learn how to import a CD, see the section "Import Tracks from a Music CD."*

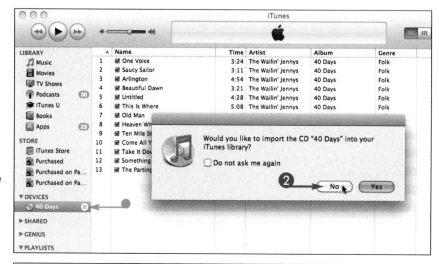

● If you have an Internet connection, iTunes shows the contents of the CD.

Note: *iTunes shows the contents for most CDs, but it may not show the correct information for some discs, particularly noncommercial mixed CDs.*

3 Click ▶.

  iTunes begins playing the CD from the first track.

Skip a Track

④ Click the **Next** button (⏭) to skip to the next track.

Note: *You can also skip to the next track by pressing ⌘+→.*

⑤ Click the **Previous** button (⏮) to skip to the beginning of the current track; click ⏮ again to skip to the previous track.

Note: *You can also skip to the previous track by pressing ⌘+←.*

Pause and Resume Play

⑥ Click ⏸ (⏸ changes to ▶).

iTunes pauses playback.

⑦ Click ▶.

iTunes resumes playback where you left off.

TIPS

Can I change the CD's audio levels?

Yes, iTunes has a graphic equalizer component that you can use to adjust the levels. To display the equalizer, click **Window** and then click **Equalizer** (or press Option +

⌘+2). In the Equalizer window, use the sliders to set the audio levels, or click the pop-up menu (▾) to choose an audio preset.

Can I display visualizations during playback?

Yes. You can click **View** and then click **Show Visualizer** (you can also press ⌘+T). To change the currently displayed visualizer, click **View**, click **Visualizer**, and then click the visualization you want to view.

iTunes gives you more options for controlling the CD playback. For example, you can switch to another song, set the CD to repeat, and play the tracks randomly. When the CD is done, you can use iTunes to eject it from your Mac.

Play a Music CD *(continued)*

Play Another Song

8 In the list of songs, double-click the song you want to play.

iTunes begins playing the song.

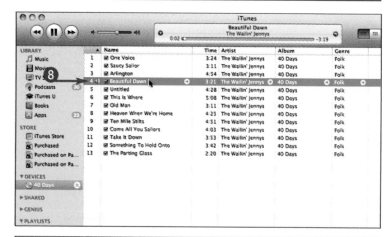

Repeat the CD

9 Click the **Repeat** button (changes to).

iTunes restarts the CD after the last track finishes playing.

To repeat just the current song, click again (changes to).

Play Songs Randomly

⑩ Click the **Shuffle** button
(⤬ changes to ⤬).

iTunes shuffles the order of play.

Eject the CD

⑪ Click the **Eject** button (⏏) beside
the CD.

Note: *You can also eject the CD by pressing and
holding the ⏏ key on the keyboard.*

iTunes ejects the CD from your
Mac's CD or DVD drive.

Why do I not see the song titles after I insert my music CD?

When you play a music CD, iTunes tries to gather information about the
album from the Internet. If you still see only track numbers, it may be that
you do not have an Internet connection established or that you inserted a
noncommercial, mixed CD. Connect to the Internet, click **Advanced**, and
then click **Get CD Track Names**.

Import Tracks from a Music CD

You can add tracks from a music CD to the iTunes Library. This enables you to listen to an album without having to put the CD into your Mac's CD or DVD drive each time. The process of adding tracks from a CD is called *importing*, or *ripping*, in Mac OS X.

After you import the tracks from a music CD, you can play those tracks from the Music category of the iTunes Library.

Import Tracks from a Music CD

① Insert a CD into your Mac's CD or DVD drive.

● The music CD appears in iTune's Devices category.

  iTunes asks if you want to import the CD.

② Click **No**.

● If you want to import the entire CD, click **Yes** and skip the rest of the steps in this section.

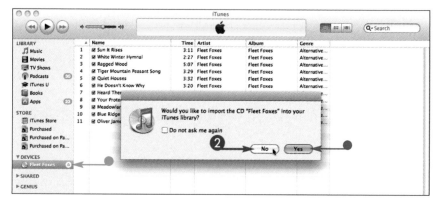

● iTunes shows the contents of the CD.

③ Click the check box so it is unchecked next to each CD track that you do not want to copy (☑ changes to ☐).

④ Click **Import CD**.

iTunes begins importing the check-marked track or tracks.

- This area displays the copy progress for each track.

- When iTunes is importing a track, it displays ⊙ beside the track number.

- When iTunes is finished importing a track, it displays ⊙ beside the track number.

- When iTunes has completed the import, you see ⊙ beside the track numbers of all the tracks you selected.

5 Click the **Eject** button (⏏) beside the CD, or press ⏏.

 TIPS

I ripped a track by accident. How do I remove it from the Library?
Click the **Music** category, open the album you imported, Control +click or right-click the track that you want to remove, and then click **Delete** from the shortcut menu. When iTunes asks you to confirm the deletion, click **Remove**. When iTunes asks if you want to keep the file, click **Move to Trash**.

Can I specify a different quality when importing?
Yes. You do that by changing the *bit rate*, which is a measure of how much of the CD's original data gets copied to your computer. This is measured in kilobits per second (Kbps): The higher the value, the higher the quality, but the more disk space each track takes up. Click **iTunes**, click **Preferences**, click **Advanced**, and then click **Importing**. In the **Settings** pop-up menu, click ⬦, click **Custom**, and then use the Stereo Bit Rate pop-up to click the value you want.

Create a Playlist

A *playlist* is a collection of songs that are related in some way. Using your iTunes Library, you can create customized playlists that include only the songs that you want to hear.

Create the Playlist

1 Click **File**.

2 Click **New Playlist**.

Note: *You can also choose the New Playlist command by pressing* ⌘ + N .

● iTunes creates a new playlist.

3 Type a name for the new playlist.

4 Press Return .

Add Songs to the Playlist

1 Click **Music**.

2 Click **List View** (▤).

3 **Control** +click or right-click a song that you want to add to the new playlist.

4 Click **Add to Playlist**.

5 Click the playlist you just created.

6 Repeat Steps **3** to **5** to add more songs to the playlist.

7 Click the playlist.

● iTunes displays the songs you added to the playlist.

● If you want to listen to the playlist, click ▶.

TIPS

Is there a faster way to create and populate a playlist?

Yes. First, click **Music** to open the Music category of the iTunes Library. Press and hold the ⌘ key and then click each song that you want to include in your playlist. When you are done, click **File** and then click **New Playlist from Selection**. (You can also press **Shift** + ⌘ + **N**.) Type the new playlist name and then press **Return**.

Is there any way to make iTunes add songs to a playlist automatically?

Yes, you can create a *smart playlist* where the songs that appear in the list have one or more properties in common, such as the genre, rating, artist, or text in the song title. Click **File** and then click **New Smart Playlist**. (You can also press **Option** + ⌘ + **N**.) Use the Smart Playlist dialog to create one or more rules that define which songs you want to appear in the playlist.

Burn Music Files to a CD

You can copy, or *burn*, music files from your Mac onto a CD. Burning CDs is a great way to create customized CDs that you can listen to on the computer or in a portable device. You can burn music files from within the iTunes window.

To burn music files to a CD, your Mac must have a recordable CD or DVD drive.

Burn Music Files to a CD

① Insert a blank CD into your Mac's recordable disc drive.

② If you already have iTunes running and your Mac asks you to choose an action, click **Ignore**.

● If you do not yet have iTunes running, use the **Action** menu to click ⬍, click **Open iTunes**, and then click **OK**.

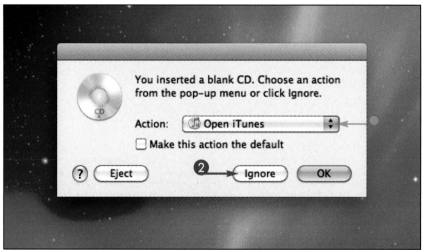

iTunes displays instructions for burning a CD.

③ Click **OK**.

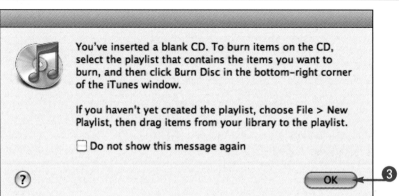

④ Create a playlist for the songs you want to burn to the disc.

Note: See the section "Create a Playlist" to learn how to build an iTunes playlist.

⑤ Click the playlist that you want to burn.

⑥ Click the heading of the play order column to ensure the songs are sorted in the order they will play on the disc.

⑦ To modify the play order, click and drag a song and drop it on a new position in the playlist.

⑧ Repeat Step **7** to get the songs in the order in which you want them to appear on the CD.

● To arrange the songs randomly, click **iTunes Shuffle** (⤫).

⑨ Click **Burn Disc**.

iTunes burns the songs to the CD.

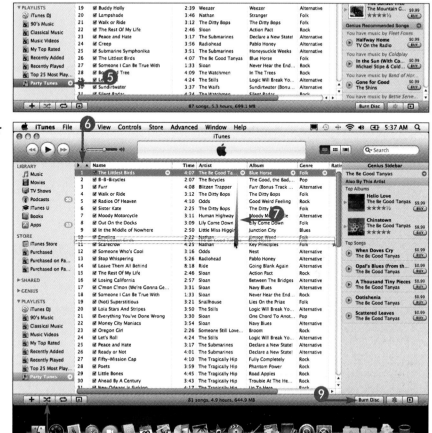

Can I control the interval between songs on the CD?

Yes. By default, iTunes adds 2 seconds between each track on the CD. To change that, click **iTunes**, click **Preferences**, click **Advanced**, and then click **Burning**. In the Gap Between Songs pop-up menu, click ⬍, and then click the interval you want to use. Click **OK**.

What happens if I have more music than can fit on a single disc?

You can still add all the music you want to burn to the playlist. iTunes fills the first disc and then adds the remaining songs to a second disc. After iTunes finishes burning the first disc, it prompts you to insert the next one.

Edit Song Information

For each song in your Library or a music CD, iTunes maintains a collection of information that includes the song title, artist, album title, genre, and more. If a song's information contains errors or omissions, you can edit the data.

You can edit one song at a time, or you can edit multiple songs, such as an entire music CD.

Edit Song Information

Edit a Single Song

1 Click the song you want to edit.

2 Click **File**.

3 Click **Get Info**.

Note: You can also press ⌘ + I . Alternatively, Control +click or right-click the song and then click **Get Info**.

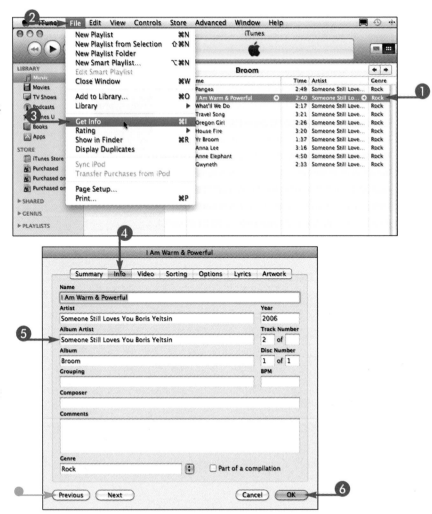

4 Click **Info**.

5 Edit or add information to the fields.

● If you want to edit a nearby song, click **Previous** or **Next** to display the song you want.

6 Click **OK**.

Edit Multiple Songs

① Select all the songs that you want to edit.

Note: To select individual songs, press and hold ⌘ and click each song; to select all songs (on a music CD, for example), press ⌘ + A .

② Click **File**.

③ Click **Get Info**.

Note: You can also press ⌘ + I . Alternatively, Control +click or right-click any selected song and then click Get Info.

iTunes asks you to confirm that you want to edit multiple songs.

④ Click **Yes**.

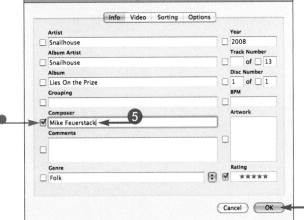

The Multiple Item Information dialog appears.

⑤ Edit or add information to the fields.

● iTunes displays ☑ beside each modified field.

⑥ Click **OK**.

iTunes applies the edits to each selected song.

TIP

When I edit multiple songs, why do I not see all the fields in the Multiple Item Information dialog?

When you are editing multiple songs, you can only modify fields that contain data that is common to all the songs. This makes sense because any changes you make apply to all the selected songs. For example, each song usually has a different title, so you would not want to give every song the same title. This is why you do not see the Name field in the Multiple Item Information dialog. However, you do see fields that are common to all the selected songs. On a music CD, for example, data such as the artist, album title, and genre are usually the same for all the songs.

Purchase Music from the iTunes Store

You can add music to your iTunes Library by purchasing songs or albums from the iTunes Store. iTunes downloads the song or album to your computer and then adds it to both the Music section and the Purchased section.

To purchase music from the iTunes Store, you must have an Apple account. This can either be an account on the Apple Store site or a MobileMe account. You can also use an AOL account, if you have one.

Purchase Music from the iTunes Store

① Click **iTunes Store**.

② Click **Music**.

The iTunes Store appears.

③ Locate the music you want to purchase.

● You can use the Search box to search for an artist, album, or song.

④ Click **Buy Album**.

● If you want to purchase just a song, click the song's **Buy** button instead.

iTunes asks you to confirm the purchase.

⑤ If you have not signed in to your account, you must type your password.

⑥ Click **Buy**.

iTunes asks you to confirm your purchase.

⑦ Click **Buy**.

iTunes charges your credit card and begins downloading the music to your Mac.

● To watch the progress of the download, click **Downloads**.

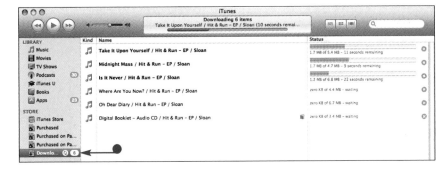

Can I use my purchased music on other computers and devices?

Yes. Although many iTunes Store media — particularly movies and TV shows — have digital rights management (DRM) restrictions applied to prevent illegal copying, the songs and albums in the iTunes Store are DRM-free, and so do not have these restrictions. This means you can play them on multiple computers and media devices (such as iPods, iPads, and iPhones), and burn them to multiple CDs.

Listen to an Internet Radio Station

The Internet offers a number of radio stations that you can listen to. iTunes maintains a list of many of these online radio stations, so it is often easier to use iTunes to listen to Internet radio.

Just like a regular radio station, an Internet radio station broadcasts a constant audio stream, except you access the audio over the Internet instead of over the air.

Listen to an Internet Radio Station

① Click **Radio**.

Note: *If you do not see the Radio category, see the first Tip on the next page.*

iTunes displays a list of radio genres.

② Click ▶ to open the genre you want to work with (▶ changes to ▼).

iTunes displays a list of radio station streams in the genre.

③ Click the radio station stream you want to listen to.

④ Click ▶.

iTunes plays the radio station stream.

● The name of the station and the name of the currently playing track usually appear here.

 TIPS

The Radio section of the iTunes Library does not appear. Can I still listen to Internet radio?

Yes. By default, iTunes does not show all of the available library categories and sources. To display the Radio source, click **iTunes** and then click **Preferences** to open the iTunes preferences. Click the **General** tab, click **Radio** (☐ changes to ☑), and then click **OK**.

Is it possible to use iTunes to save or record a song from a radio station stream?

No, an Internet radio stream is "listen-only." iTunes does not give you any way to save the stream to your Mac hard disk or to record the stream as it plays.

Subscribe to a Podcast

A *podcast* is an audio feed — or sometimes a feed that combines both audio and video — that a publisher updates regularly with new episodes. The easiest way to get each episode is to subscribe to the podcast. This ensures that iTunes automatically downloads each new episode to your iTunes Library.

You can subscribe to podcasts either directly via the publisher's Web site, or via the iTunes Store.

Subscribe to a Podcast

Subscribe to a Podcast on the Web

1. Use your Web browser to navigate to the podcast's home page.

2. Click the **Subscribe in iTunes** link.

Note: *In some cases, the link is called **Add to iTunes** or simply **iTunes**.*

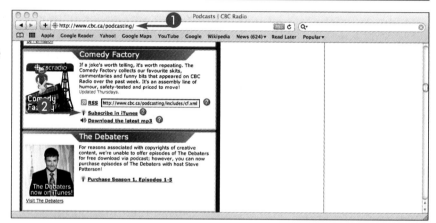

● iTunes begins downloading the available episodes.

● The podcast subscription appears in the Library's Podcasts category.

Subscribe to a Podcast Using the iTunes Store

1 Click **iTunes Store**.

2 Click **Podcasts**.

● You can also click here to display a list of podcast categories.

3 Locate the podcast you want to subscribe to.

4 Click **Subscribe Free**.

● If you just want to listen to one episode before subscribing, click the episode's **Free** button instead.

iTunes begins downloading the podcast.

To listen to the podcast, click the subscription in the Podcasts category of the Library.

What do I do if the podcast Web site does not have an iTunes link?
In this case, you can subscribe to the podcast by telling iTunes the address of the podcast's feed. Follow these steps:

1 On the podcast Web site, copy the address of the podcast feed.

2 In iTunes, click **Advanced**.

3 Click **Subscribe to Podcast**.

The Subscribe to Podcast dialog appears.

4 Use the **URL** text box to paste (or type) the address of the podcast feed.

5 Click **OK**.

iTunes downloads the available episodes and adds the subscription to the Podcasts category of the Library.

CHAPTER 6

Viewing and Editing Your Photos

Whether you just want to look at your photos, or you want to edit your photos to crop out unneeded portions or fix problems, Mac OS X comes with a number of useful tools for working with your photos. If your Mac comes with the iLife suite, you can also use iPhoto to view and edit photos.

View a Preview of a Photo

You can preview a saved image file using the Mac OS X Quick Look feature or the Cover Flow view. You can also preview photos using the Preview application.

View a Preview with Quick Look

1. Click **Finder** (⬛) in the Dock.

2. Open the folder that contains the photo you want to preview.

3. Click the photo.

4. Click **Quick Look** (👁).

   You can also select Quick Look by pressing Spacebar.

● Finder displays a preview of the photo.

View a Preview with Cover Flow

1. Click **Finder** (⬛) in the Dock.

2. Open the folder that contains the photo you want to preview.

3. Click the photo.

4. Click **Cover Flow** (▦).

● Finder displays a preview of the photo.

● Use the scroll bar to scroll through the other photos in the folder.

View a Preview in the Preview Application

1 Click **Finder** () in the Dock.

2 Open the folder that contains the photo you want to preview.

3 Click the photo.

4 Click **File**.

5 Click **Open With**.

6 Click **Preview**.

Note: In many cases, you can also simply double-click the photo to open it in the Preview application.

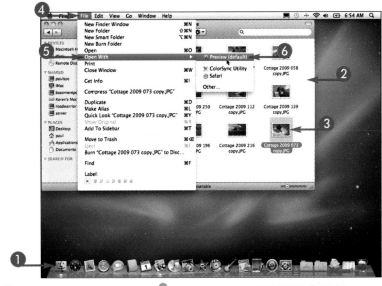

The Preview application opens and displays the photo.

7 Use the toolbar buttons to change how the photo appears in the Preview window. For example, click **Zoom +** to get a closer look at the photos.

● More commands are available on the **View** menu.

8 When you are finished viewing the photo, click **Close** ().

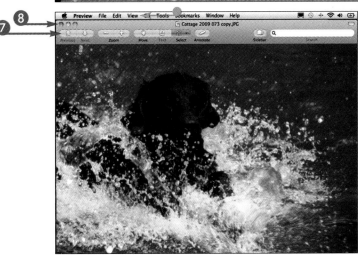

TIPS

Is there an easier way to preview multiple photos using the Preview application?

Yes. Instead of constantly starting and quitting Preview for each photo you want to view, you can load multiple photos into the Preview application. In Finder, navigate to the folder that contains the photos, and then select each file that you want to preview. Either click and drag the mouse (k) over the photos or press and hold ⌘ and click each one. In Preview, click **Next** and **Previous** to navigate the photos.

Is there a way that I can zoom in on just a portion of a photo?

Yes. In Preview, click **Tools** and then click **Select Tool** (or either press ⌘+3 or click **Select** in the toolbar). Click and drag your mouse (k) to select the portion of the photo that you want to magnify. Click **View** and then click **Zoom to Selection** (or press ⌘+*).

View a Slide Show of Your Photos

You can easily view multiple photos by running them in a slide show using the Mac OS X Quick Look feature. The slide show automatically displays the next photo after a few seconds, and you can view the images full-screen.

① Click **Finder** (⬚) in the Dock.

② Open the folder that contains the photos you want to view in the slide show.

③ Select the photos you want to view.

④ Click **Quick Look** (👁).

You can also select Quick Look by pressing Spacebar.

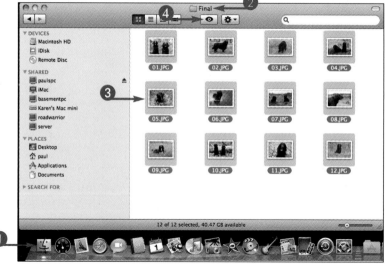

The Quick Look window appears.

⑤ Click **Play**.

⑥ Click **Full Screen**.

Quick Look begins the slide show.

7 Move the mouse (↖).

● Preview displays the slide show controls.

● Click **Next** to move to the next photo.

● Click **Back** to move to the previous photo.

● Click **Pause** to suspend the slide show.

8 When the slide show is over or when you want to return to Finder, click **Close** or press Esc.

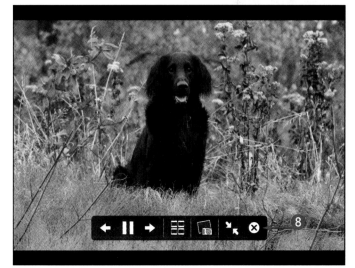

Is it possible to jump to a specific photo during the slide show?

Yes, by using the Index Sheet feature. In the slide show controls, click the **Index Sheet** button, which is the icon with the four rectangles arranged in a grid. Preview displays thumbnail views of all the slide show images. Click the photo that you want to view in the slide show.

What keyboard shortcuts can I use when viewing a slide show?

Press ➡ to display the next photo, and press ⬅ to display the previous photo. Press Spacebar to pause the slide show, and press Spacebar to resume. Press Esc to end the slide show.

Open and Close iPhoto

Mac OS X includes iPhoto to enable you to import photos from a digital camera, as well as to view, organize, share, edit, and repair photos. To begin using the program, you must first learn how to find and open the iPhoto window. When you finish using the program, you can close the iPhoto window to free up computer processing power.

Open iPhoto

① Click **Finder** (⬛) in the Dock.

② Click **Applications**.

③ Double-click **iPhoto**.

The iPhoto window appears.

The first time you launch iPhoto, the program asks if you want to use iPhoto when you connect your digital camera.

④ Click **Yes**.

The first time you launch iPhoto, the program asks if you want to view your photos on a map.

⑤ If you have a GPS-enabled camera (such as an iPhone 4, 3GS, or 3G) or if you want to enter location data by hand, click **Yes**.

Close iPhoto

1 Click **iPhoto**.

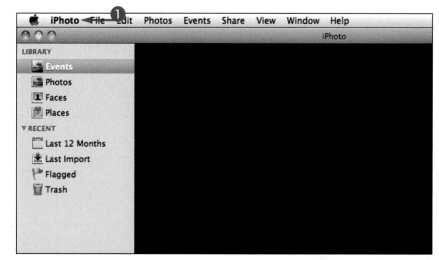

2 Click **Quit iPhoto**.

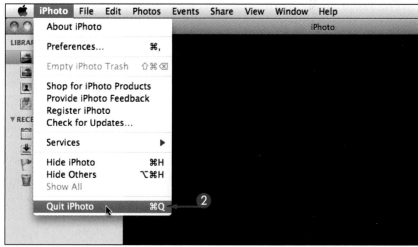

Are there faster methods I can use to open iPhoto?

The fastest way to start iPhoto is to click the **iPhoto** icon (🖼) in the Dock. If you have used iPhoto recently, another reasonably fast method is to click 🍎, click **Recent Items**, and then click **iPhoto**.

Are there faster methods I can use to close iPhoto?

Probably the fastest method you can use to quit iPhoto is to click 🔴. Alternatively, Control +click or right-click the **iPhoto** icon (🖼) and then click **Quit**. Finally, if your hands are closer to the keyboard than to the mouse, you can quit iPhoto by pressing ⌘+Q.

Import Photos from a Digital Camera

You can import photos from a digital camera and save them on your Mac. Snow Leopard uses the iPhoto application to handle importing photos.

You will need a cable to connect your digital camera to your Mac. Most digital cameras come with a USB cable.

Import Photos from the Digital Camera

1. Connect one end of the cable to the digital camera.

2. Connect the other end of the cable to a free USB port on your Mac.

3. Turn the camera on and put it in either playback or computer mode.

   Your Mac launches the iPhoto application.

- Your digital camera appears in the Devices section.

- iPhoto displays previews of the camera's photos.

4. Use the Event Name text box to type a name for the group of photos you are going to import.

5. Use the Description text box to type a description of the photos you are going to import.

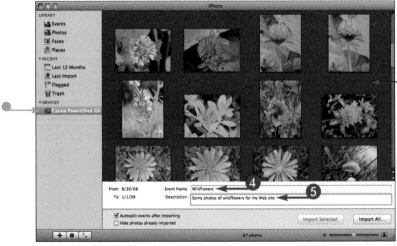

6 Select the photos that you want to import.

Note: To select photos, either click and drag the mouse (▶) around the photos you want, or press and hold ⌘ and click each photo.

7 Click **Import Selected**.

● If you want to import all the photos from the digital camera, click **Import All** instead.

iPhoto imports the photos from the digital camera.

iPhoto asks if you want to delete the original photos from the digital camera.

8 If you no longer need the photos on the camera, click **Delete Photos**.

● If you prefer to keep the photos on the camera, click **Keep Photos** instead.

View the Imported Photos

1 Click **Events**.

2 Double-click the event name that you specified in Step **4** on the previous page.

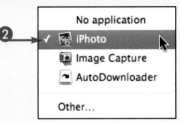

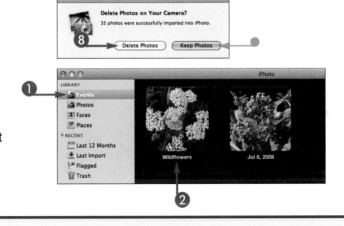

When I connect my digital camera, why do I see Image Capture instead of iPhoto?
You need to configure Image Capture to open iPhoto when you connect your camera. Follow these steps:

1 Connect your digital camera to your Mac.

The Image Capture application opens.

*Note: If you do not see the Image Capture application, click **Finder** (🖥) in the Dock, click **Applications**, and then double-click **Image Capture**.*

2 Click the **When connected, launch** 🔅 and then click **iPhoto**.

3 Click **Image Capture** in the menu bar.

4 Click **Quit Image Capture**.

> No application
> ✓ 📷 iPhoto
> 📷 Image Capture
> 📄 AutoDownloader
>
> Other...

View Your Photos

If you want to look at several photos, you can use iPhoto's full-screen mode to navigate backward and forward through the photos in a folder.

1. In iPhoto, click **Events**.

2. Double-click the event that contains the photos you want to view.

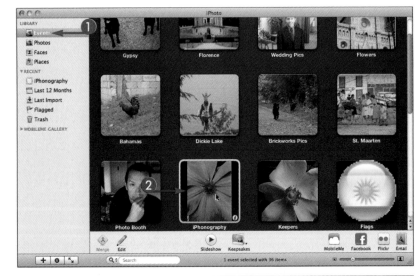

3. Click the first photo you want to view.

4. Click **Enter full screen** (⬜).

iPhoto displays the photo in full-screen mode.

5 Move the mouse (↖) to the bottom of the screen.

iPhoto displays the full-screen controls.

6 Click **Next** (▶) to view the next photo in the event.

● You can also click **Previous** (◀) to see the previous photo in the event.

Note: *You can also navigate photos by pressing* → *and* ←.

7 When you are done, move the mouse (↖) to the bottom of the screen.

8 Click **Exit** (✕) or press Esc.

TIP

Is there a way that I can jump quickly to a particular photo in full-screen mode?
Yes. Follow these steps:

1 Move the mouse (↖) to the top of the screen.

● iPhoto displays thumbnail images of the Event's photos.

2 Use the horizontal scroll bar to bring the thumbnail of the photo you want into view.

3 Click the photo's thumbnail.

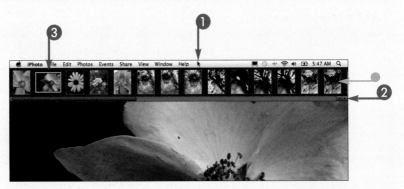

Create an Album

An *album* is a collection of photos that are related in some way. Using your iPhoto Library, you can create customized albums that include only the photos that you want to view.

Create the Album

① Click **File**.

② Click **New Album**.

Note: You can also choose the New Album command by pressing ⌘ + N.

③ Type a name for the new album.

④ Click **Create**.

Add Photos to the Album

1 Click **Photos**.

2 Click ▶ beside the event that contains the photos you want to work with (▶ changes to ▼).

3 Click and drag a photo and drop it on the new album.

4 Repeat Steps **2** and **3** to add other photos to the album.

5 Click the album.

● iPhoto displays the photos you added to the album.

TIPS

Is there a faster way to create and populate an album?

Yes. First, click **Photos** to open the Photos section of the iPhoto Library, and then open the event you want to work with. Press and hold the ⌘ key and then click each photo that you want to include in your album. When you are done, click **File** and then click **New Album from Selection**. (You can also press Shift + ⌘ + N.) Type the new album name and then click **Create**.

Is there any way to make iPhoto add photos to an album automatically?

Yes, you can create a *smart album* where the photos that appear in the album have one or more properties in common, such as the description, rating, date, or text in the photo title. Click **File** and then click **New Smart Album**. (You can also press Option + ⌘ + N.) Use the Smart Album dialog to create one or more rules that define which photos you want to appear in the album.

If you have a photo containing elements that you do not want or need to see, you can often cut out those elements. This is called *cropping*, and it can help give focus to the true subject of a photo.

When you crop a photo, you specify a rectangular area of the photo that you want to keep. iPhoto discards everything outside of the rectangle.

Crop a Photo

1 Click the photo you want to crop.

2 Click **Edit** (✎).

iPhoto displays its editing tools.

3 Click **Crop** (▫).

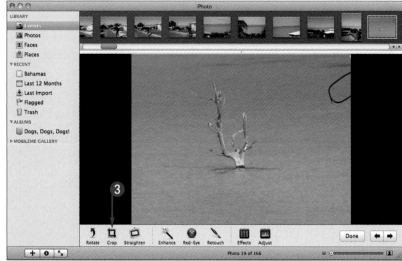

iPhoto displays a cropping rectangle on the photo.

4 Click and drag a corner or side to define the area you want to keep.

Note: *Remember that iPhoto keeps the area inside the rectangle.*

5 Click **Apply**.

iPhoto saves the cropped photo.

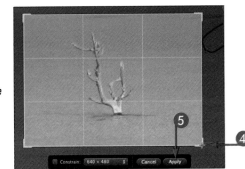

6 Click **Done**.

iPhoto exits edit mode.

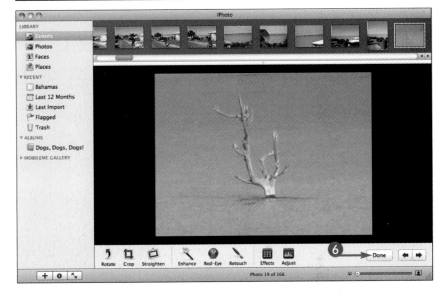

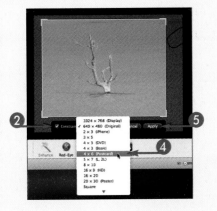

TIP

Is there a quick way to crop a photo to a certain size?
Yes, iPhoto enables you to specify either a specific size, such as 640 × 480, or a specific ratio, such as 4 × 3 or 16 × 9. Follow these steps:

1 Follow Steps **1** to **3** to display the Crop tool.

2 Click the **Constrain** check box (☐ changes to ☑).

3 In the Constrain list, click ⬦.

4 Click the size or ratio you want to use.

5 Click **Apply**.

Rotate a Photo

If you have a photo that shows the subject sideways or upside down, you can use iPhoto to rotate the photo so that the subject appears right-side up. You can rotate a photo either clockwise or counterclockwise.

① Click the photo you want to rotate.

② Click **Rotate** (🔄).

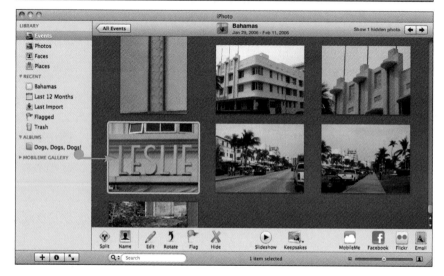

● iPhoto rotates the photo 90 degrees counterclockwise.

③ Repeat Step **2** until the subject of the photo is right-side up.

If you want to rotate the photo clockwise instead, press and hold the Option key and then click 🔄.

If you have an event or album that contains a photo that you do not like or that is very similar to another image in the same event or album, you can hide the photo. This makes the event or album easier to navigate and view.

Hide a Photo

1 Click the photo you want to hide.

2 Click **Hide** ([X]).

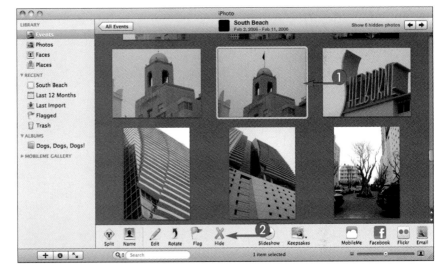

● iPhoto removes the photo from the event or album.

To view a hidden photo, click **View** and then click **Hidden Photos**.

Straighten a Photo

If you have a photo that is not quite level, you can use iPhoto to nudge the photo clockwise or counterclockwise so that the subject appears straight.

Straighten a Photo

1 Click the photo you want to straighten.

2 Click **Edit** (✐).

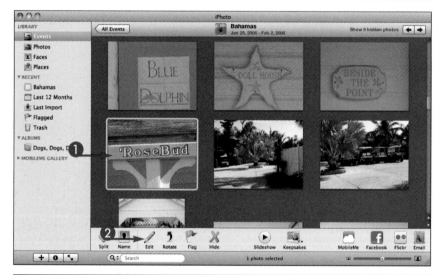

iPhoto displays its editing tools.

3 Click **Straighten** (▱).

iPhoto displays a grid over the photo.

④ Click and drag the **Change angle of photo** slider.

Drag the slider to the left to angle the photo counterclockwise.

Drag the slider to the right to angle the photo clockwise.

⑤ Click **Done**.

iPhoto exits edit mode.

How do I know when my photo is level?

Use the gridlines that iPhoto places over the photo. Locate a horizontal line in your photo, and then rotate the photo so that this line is parallel to the nearest horizontal line in the grid. You can also match a vertical line in the photo with a vertical line in the grid.

Remove Red Eye from a Photo

If you have a photo where one or more people have red eyes due to the camera flash, you can use iPhoto to remove the red eye and give your subjects a more natural look.

① Click the photo that contains the red eye.

② Click **Edit** (✐).

iPhoto displays its editing tools.

③ Click **Red-Eye** (◉).

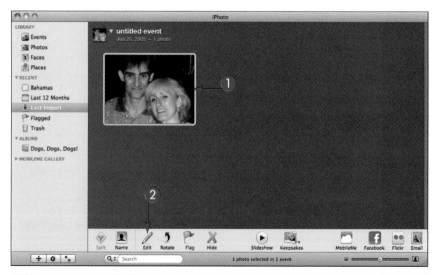

iPhoto displays its Red-Eye controls.

● If needed, you can click and drag this slider to the right to zoom in on the picture.

④ Click and drag this rectangle to bring the red eye into view.

⑤ Click the red eye in the photo.

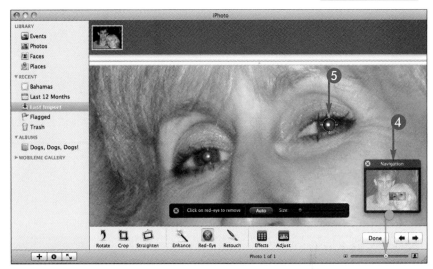

● iPhoto removes the red eye.

⑥ Repeat Step **5** to fix any other instances of red eye in the photo.

⑦ Click ☒ (or click ◉) to exit the Red-Eye tool.

⑧ Click **Done**.

iPhoto exits edit mode.

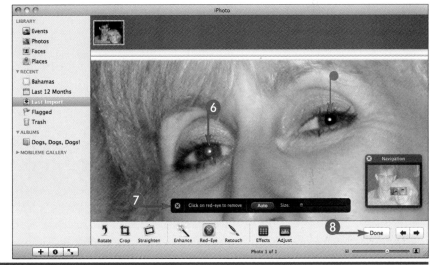

TIP

Why does iPhoto remove only part of the red eye in my photo when I click it with the Red-Eye tool?

The Red-Eye tool may not be large enough. The tool should be approximately the same size as the subject's eye:

① Follow Steps **1** to **4** to display the Red-Eye controls and bring the red eye into view.

② Click and drag the **Size** slider until the Red-Eye tool is the size of the red-eye area.

③ Use your mouse to move the circle over the red eye and then click.

iPhoto removes the red eye that occurs within the circle.

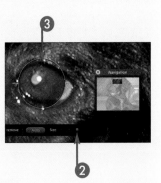

Add Names to Faces in Your Photos

You can annotate your photos by adding names to the faces that appear in them. This enables you to navigate your photos by name. For example, you can view all your photos in which a certain person appears.

To add names to the faces in your photos, you must be using iPhoto '09 or later. To check this, click iPhoto in the menu bar and then click About iPhoto.

① Click the photo that you want to annotate.

② Click **Name** (🖼).

iPhoto displays its naming tools.

③ Click **unnamed**.

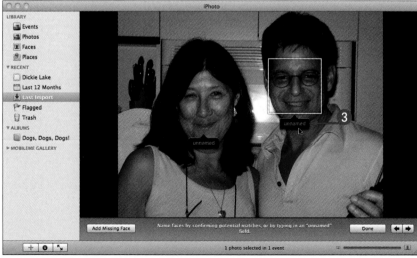

④ Type the person's name.

⑤ Press **Return**.

⑥ Repeat Steps **3** to **5** to name each person in the photo.

● If iPhoto did not mark a face in the photo, click **Add Missing Face**, size and position the box over the face, click **Done**, and then follow Steps **3** to **5**.

⑦ Click **Done**.

iPhoto exits naming mode.

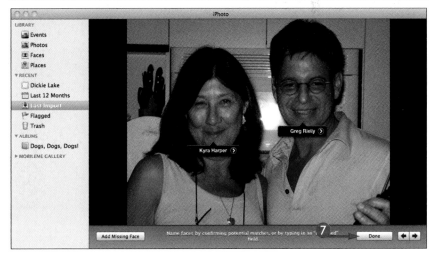

TIP

How do I view all the photos that contain a particular person?

One method you can use is to open a photo, click 🔲, and then click the **Show All** arrow (▶) that appears beside the person's name. You can also follow these steps:

① Click **Faces** in the iPhoto sidebar.

● iPhoto displays the names and sample photos of each person you have named.

② Double-click the person you want to view.

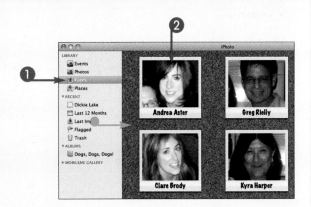

You can tell iPhoto the locations where your photos were taken, and then display a map that shows those locations. This enables you to view all your photos taken in a particular place.

To map your photos, you must be using iPhoto '09 or later. To check this, click iPhoto in the menu bar and then click About iPhoto.

Map Your Photos

① Position the ⬈ over the event that you want to map.

If you want to map a single photo, open the event and position the ⬈ over the photo.

② Click the **Information** icon (⬤).

iPhoto displays the Information window.

③ Click **event place**.

④ Click **Find on map**.

The Add New Place window appears.

⑤ Type the location and then press Return.

iPhoto displays the location on a Google map.

⑥ Click and drag the pin to the correct location, if necessary.

⑦ Click **Add** (➕).

iPhoto adds the location to the My Places tab.

⑧ Click **Assign to event**.

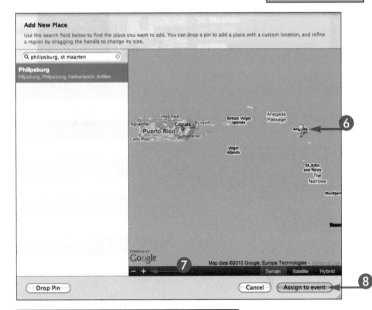

⑨ Click **Done**.

iPhoto closes the information window.

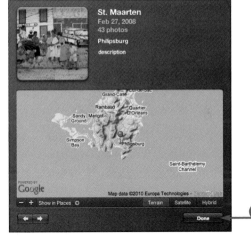

Is there a way to have the location data added automatically?

Yes. If you have a GPS-enabled phone — such as an iPhone 3G or later — iPhoto automatically picks up location data from the photos. However, for this to work, you must activate this feature. Click **iPhoto** in the menu bar, click **Preferences**, and then click the **Advanced** tab. Click the **Look up Places** 🔽 and then click **Automatically**. Note that you may still have to add or edit location names for your photos.

How do I view all the photos that were taken in a particular place?

Click **Places** in the iPhoto sidebar to see a map of the world with pins for each of your photo locations. Position the mouse (🔦) over the location's pin, and then click the **Show All** arrow (▶). iPhoto displays all the photos that were taken in that location.

If you have a photo that you want to share with someone, and you know that person's e-mail address, you can send the photo in an e-mail message.

Even if a photo is very large, you can still send it via e-mail because you can use iPhoto to shrink the copy of the photo that appears in the message.

E-Mail a Photo

① Click the photo you want to send.

② Click **Share**.

③ Click **Email**.

● You can also click **Email** (⬜).

The Mail 1 Photo dialog appears.

4 In the Size list, click ⬍ and then click the size you want to use for the sent photo.

5 Click **Compose Message**.

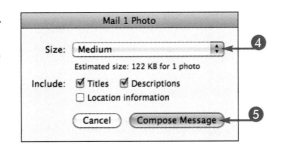

iPhoto creates a new Mail message.

● The photo appears in the message body.

6 Use the To text box to type the address of the message recipient.

7 Use the Subject text box to type the message subject.

8 Click **Send**.

Apple Mail sends the message.

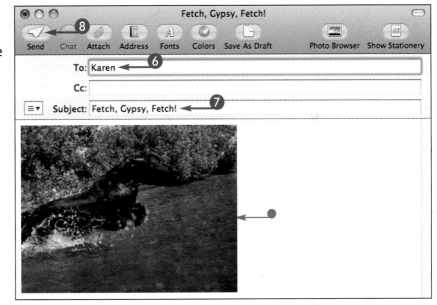

TIP

How do I insert some text above the photo?

Inserting a bit of text above the photo is a good idea because it enables you to introduce the photo and let the recipient know why you are sending it. To add the text, follow these steps:

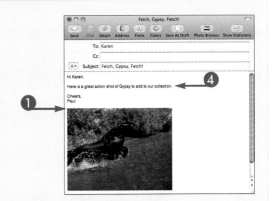

1 Click inside the narrow white area to the left of the photo.

   Apple Mail displays a large, blinking cursor to the left of the photo.

2 Press Return.

3 Press ⬆.

   The cursor moves into the new line you created.

4 Type your message above the photo.

Take Your Picture

If your Mac comes with a built-in iSight camera, or if you have an external camera attached to your Mac, you can use the camera to take a picture of yourself using the Photo Booth application.

Once you have taken your picture, you can e-mail that picture, add it to iPhoto, or set is as your user account or iChat buddy picture.

Take Your Picture with Photo Booth

1 In the Dock, click **Photo Booth** (▦).

The Photo Booth window appears.

● The live feed from the camera appears here.

2 Click **Take a still picture** (▢).

● Click **Take four quick pictures** (▦) if you want Photo Booth to snap four successive photos, each about 1 second apart.

● Click **Take a movie clip** (▤) if you want Photo Booth to capture the live camera feed as a movie.

③ Click **Take Photo** (◉).

Note: *You can also press* ⌘ *+* T *or click* **File** *and then click* **Take Photo**.

Photo Booth counts down 3 seconds and then takes the photo.

Note: *When the Mac is taking your picture, be sure to look into the camera, not into the screen.*

Work with Your Photo Booth Picture

● Photo Booth displays the picture.

① Click the taken picture.

● Click **Email** (▣) to send the photo in an e-mail message.

● Click **iPhoto** (▣) to add the photo to iPhoto.

● Click **Account Picture** (▣) to set the photo as your user account picture.

● Click **Buddy Picture** (▣) to set the photo as your iChat buddy picture.

TIP

Can I make my photos more interesting?
Definitely. Photo Booth comes with around two dozen special effects that can make your photo look like an x-ray or comic book, apply distortions such as a mirror image, add a background image, and more. Follow these steps:

① In Photo Booth, click **Effects**.

② Click an icon to select a different page of effects.

● You can also use the arrow buttons to change pages.

③ Click the effect you want to use.

CHAPTER 7

Playing and Creating Digital Video

Your Mac comes with the tools you need to play movies and digital video as well as to create your own digital video movies. Using the iMovie application that comes with the iLife suite, you can import camcorder video; apply scene transitions; add titles, credits, and a soundtrack; and even export your movie to a DVD.

Play a DVD Using DVD Player

If your Mac has a DVD drive, you can use the DVD Player application to play a DVD movie. You can either watch the movie in full-screen mode, or you can play the DVD in a window while you work on other things. DVD Player has features that enable you to control the movie playback and volume.

Play a DVD Using DVD Player

Play a DVD Full-Screen

1. Insert the DVD disc into your Mac's DVD drive.

   DVD Player runs automatically and starts playing the DVD full-screen.

2. If you get to the DVD menu, click **Play** to start the movie.

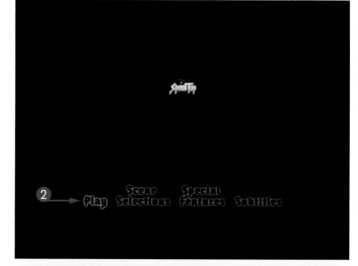

3. Move the ➤ to the bottom of the screen.

   The playback controls appear.

- Click to pause the movie.

- Click to fast-forward the movie.

- Click to rewind the movie.

- Drag the slider to adjust the volume.

- Click to display the DVD menu.

- Click to exit full-screen mode.

- Click to eject the DVD.

Play a DVD in a WIndow

1. Insert the DVD disc into your Mac's DVD drive.

   DVD Player runs automatically and starts playing the DVD full-screen.

2. Press ⌘+F.

   You can also press Esc or move the ▶ to the bottom of the screen and then click **Exit full screen**.

   DVD Player displays the movie in a window.

● DVD Player displays the Controller.

3. When you get to the DVD menu, click **Play** to start the movie.

● Click to pause the movie.

● Click and hold to fast-forward the movie.

● Click and hold to rewind the movie.

● Drag the slider to adjust the volume.

● Click to display the DVD menu.

● Click to stop the movie.

● Click to eject the DVD.

How can I always start my DVDs in a window?

1. Press ⌘+F to switch to the window view.

2. Click **DVD Player** in the menu bar.

3. Click **Preferences** to open the DVD Player preferences.

4. Click the **Player** tab.

5. Click **Enter Full Screen mode** (☑ changes to ☐).

6. If you want to control when the playback starts, also click **Start playing disc** (☑ changes to ☐).

7. Click **OK** to put the new settings into effect.

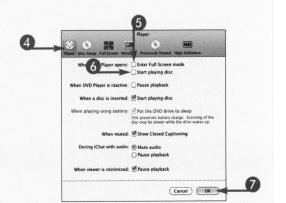

Play Digital Video with QuickTime Player

Your Mac comes with an application called QuickTime Player that can play digital video files. You will mostly use QuickTime Player to play digital video files stored on your Mac, but you can also use the application to play digital video files from the Web.

1 Click **Finder** (🖳).

2 Click **Applications**.

3 Double-click **QuickTime Player**.

The QuickTime Player window appears.

4 Click **File**.

5 Click **Open File**.

You can also press ⌘+O.

The Open dialog appears.

6 Locate and click the video file you want to play.

7 Click **Open**.

QuickTime opens a new player window.

8 Click **Play** (▶).

● Click here to fast-forward the video.

● Click here to rewind the video.

● Click and drag this slider to adjust the volume.

If you want to view the video in full-screen mode, press ⌘ + F.

 TIP

Can I use QuickTime Player to play a video from the Web?
Yes, as long as you know the Internet address of the video, QuickTime Player can play most video formats available on the Web. In QuickTime Player, click **File** and then click **Open URL** (or press ⌘ + U). In the Open URL dialog, type or paste the video address in the Movie URL text box, and then click **Open**.

Create a New Movie Project

The iLife suite includes iMovie, which enables you to import video from a digital camcorder or video file and use that footage to create your own movies. You do this by first creating a project that holds your video clips, transitions, titles, and other elements of your movie.

When you first start iMovie, the program creates a new project for you automatically. Follow the steps in this section to create subsequent projects.

Create a New Movie Project

① Click the **iMovie** icon (▣) in the Dock.

The iMovie window appears.

② Click **File**.

③ Click **New Project**.

You can also press ⌘+N.

The New Project dialog appears.

④ Use the Project Name text box to type a name for your project.

⑤ Click the **Aspect Ratio** ⬍ and then click the ratio you prefer: Widescreen (16:9), Standard (4:3), or iPhone (3:2).

⑥ If you want to apply a theme to your project, click the one you want in the Theme list.

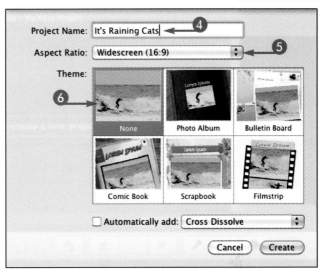

⑦ If you want iMovie to automatically insert transitions between all your clips, click **Automatically add** (☐ changes to ☑) and then click ⬍ to choose the type of transition.

If you chose a theme in Step **6**, the name of the check box changes to **Automatically add transition and titles**, and iMovie selects it by default.

⑧ Click **Create**.

iMovie creates your new project.

TIPS

What are the iMovie themes?
One of the goals of iMovie '09 is to make digital video editing as effortless as possible. To that end, iMovie '09 offers several themes that you can apply to a project. Each theme comes with its own set of titles and transitions that get added automatically, saving you lots of work.

There are five themes in all: Photo Album, Bulletin Board, Comic Book, Scrapbook, and Filmstrip. If one of them is suitable for your project, applying it cuts down on your production time.

How do I switch from one project to another?
You use the Project Library, which is a list of your movie projects. To display it, click **Window** and then click **Show Project Library**. You can also click the **Project Library** button in the top left corner of the iMovie window. In the Project Library, double-click the project you want to work with.

If you have video content on a FireWire or USB digital camcorder, you can connect the camcorder to your Mac and then import some or all of the video to your iMovie project.

The procedure described in this section applies to tape-based video cameras. If you have a camcorder that uses a disk or memory card, the procedure will be slightly different.

Import a Video File

Import all Footage

1 Connect the digital camcorder to your Mac.

iMovie displays its Import From dialog.

2 Click **Import**.

iMovie rewinds the tape to the beginning, imports all the footage, and then rewinds the tape.

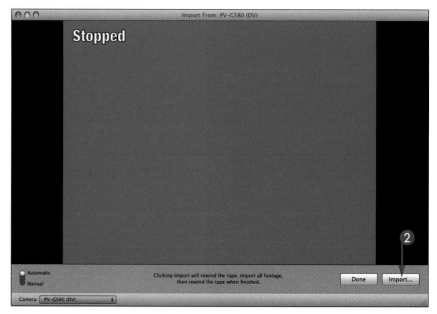

iMovie prompts you to create a new event.

3 Click **Create new Event** (○ changes to ●).

4 Use the Create new Event text box to type a name for the import event.

● If you want to add the video to an existing event, click **Add to existing Event** (○ changes to ●) and then choose the event from the pop-up menu.

5 Click **Import**.

Import Selected Footage

1 Connect the digital camcorder to your Mac.

iMovie displays its Import From dialog.

2 Click **Manual**.

3 Click **Play** (▶).

● You can click and hold **Seek Forward** (▶▶) to speed up the playback.

● If you go too far, you can click and hold **Seek Back** (◀◀) to skip back.

4 When you get to the part you want to import, click **Import**.

iMovie pauses the playback and prompts you to create a new event.

5 Click Create new Event (○ changes to ●).

6 Use the Create new Event text box to type a name for the import event.

7 Click **Import**.

iMovie begins importing the video.

*Note: To skip recording some of the tape, click **Stop** and then repeat Steps **3** to **7**. In the dialog, be sure to click **Add to existing Event** (○ changes to ●).*

8 Click **Done**.

TIP

How do I import digital video from my iSight camera?

1 In iMovie, click **File** and then click **Import from Camera**.

2 Click 🔹 and then click the frame size you want.

3 Click **Capture**.

4 Follow Steps **5** to **7** on this page.

5 When you are done, click **Stop**.

6 Click **Done**.

Add Video Clips to Your Project

A *video clip* is a segment of digital video. You begin building your movie by adding one or more video clips to your project.

When you import digital video as described in the previous section, iMovie automatically breaks up the video into separate clips, with each clip being the footage shot during a single recording session.

Add Video Clips to Your Project

Add an Entire Clip

1. Click the Event Library item that contains the video clip you want to add.

2. Press and hold `Option` and click the clip.

● iMovie selects the entire clip.

3. Click and drag the selected clip and drop it in your project at the spot where you want the clip to appear.

● iMovie adds the entire video clip to the project.

● iMovie adds an orange bar to the bottom of the original clip to indicate that it has been added to the project.

Add a Partial Clip

1 Click the Event Library item that contains the video clip you want to add.

2 Click the clip at the point where you want the selection to begin.

3 Click and drag the right edge of the selection box to the point where you want the selection to end.

4 Click and drag the selected clip and drop it in your project at the spot where you want the clip to appear.

● iMovie adds the selected portion of the video clip to the project.

● iMovie adds an orange bar to the bottom of the original clip to indicate that it has been added to a project.

TIPS

Is it possible to play a clip before I add it?

Yes. The easiest way to do this is to click the clip at the point where you want the playback to start and then press **Spacebar**. iMovie plays the clip in the Viewer in the top right corner of the window. Press **Spacebar** again to stop the playback. If you want to see only a portion of the clip, follow Steps **2** and **3** on this page to make your selection, **Control** +click or right-click the clip, and then click **Play Selection**.

I added a clip in the wrong place. Can I move it?

Yes. In your project, click the added clip to select it. Use your mouse (↖) to click and drag the clip and then drop the clip in the correct location within the project. If you want to delete the clip from the project, click it, click **Edit**, and then click **Delete Entire Clip**.

Trim a Clip

If you have a video clip that is too long contains footage you do not need, you can shorten the clip or remove the extra footage. Removing parts of a video clip is called *trimming* the clip.

Trim a Clip

① In your project, click the clip you want to trim.

● iMovie selects the entire clip.

② Use your mouse (↖) to click and drag the left edge of the selection box to the starting position of the part of the clip you want to keep.

③ Use your mouse (↖) to click and drag the right edge of the selection box to the ending position of the part of the clip you want to keep.

④ Click **Edit**.

⑤ Click **Trim to Selection**.

Note: You can also press ⌘ + B *.*

● iMovie trims the clip.

TIP

Is it possible to trim a certain number of frames from a clip?

Yes, iMovie enables you to trim up to 30 frames (1 second) at a time from either the beginning or the end of the clip. Follow these steps:

① Press and hold ⌘ and Option.

② To trim from the beginning, position the mouse (↖) at the beginning of the clip.

Note: To trim from the end, position the mouse (↖) at the end of the clip instead.

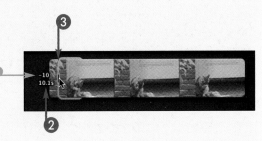

③ Use your mouse (↖) to click and drag the edge of the selection box.

● iMovie displays the number of frames you are trimming.

④ Release the mouse (↖) as well as ⌘ and Option when you reach the number of frames that you want to trim.

Add a Transition Between Clips

By default, iMovie jumps immediately from the end of one clip to the beginning of another. You can add more visual interest to your movie by adding a transition between the two clips.

iMovie offers 20 different transitions, including various fades, wipes, and dissolves.

Add a Transition Between Clips

① Click the **Transitions browser** button (▦).

● iMovie displays the available transitions.

Note: To see a preview of a transition, position your mouse (▸) over the transition thumbnail.

② Use your mouse (▸) to click and drag a transition and drop it between the two clips.

● iMovie adds an icon for the transition between the two clips.

③ Position your mouse (↖) over the beginning of the transition and move the ↖ to the right.

● iMovie displays a preview of the transition.

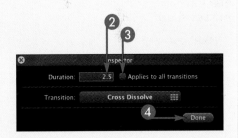

TIP

Can I change the duration of the transition?
Yes. The default length is half a second, but you can increase or decrease the duration by following these steps:

① Double-click the transition icon in your project.

 The Inspector appears.

② Use the Duration text box to set the number of seconds you want the transition to take.

③ If you want to change only the current transition, click **Applies to all transitions** (☑ changes to ☐).

④ Click **Done**.

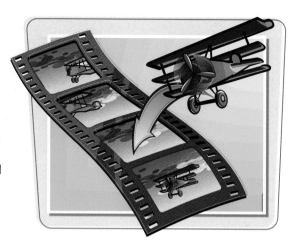

Although most movie projects consist of several video clips, you can also add a photo to your project. By default, iMovie displays the photo for 4 seconds.

You can also specify how the photo fits in the movie frame: You can adjust the size of the photo to fit the frame, you can crop the photo, or you can apply a Ken Burns effect — which automatically pans and zooms the photo — to animate the static photo.

Add a Photo

① Click the **Photos browser** button (◙).

● iMovie displays the available photos.

② Click the event or album that contains the photo you want to add.

③ Click and drag the photo and drop it inside your project.

● iMovie adds the photo to the movie.

④ Click the photo.

⑤ Click the **Crop** button (▣).

iMovie displays the cropping options for the photo.

⑥ Click **Ken Burns**.

● You can also click **Fit** to have iMovie adjust the size of the photo to fit the movie frame.

● You can also click **Crop** and then click and drag the cropping rectangle to specify how much of the photo you want to appear in the movie frame.

⑦ Click and drag the green rectangle to set the start point of the Ken Burns animation.

⑧ Click and drag the red rectangle to set the end point of the Ken Burns animation.

Note: Click and drag the corners and edges of the rectangle to change the size; click and drag the interior of the rectangles to change the position.

● The arrow shows the direction of motion.

⑨ Click **Done**.

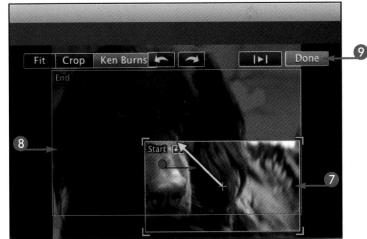

Can I change the length of time that the photo appears in the movie?

Yes. The default length is 4 seconds, but you can increase or decrease the duration by following these steps:

① Double-click the photo in your project.

② Click **Clip**.

③ Use the Duration text box to set the number of seconds you want the photo to appear.

④ To change the duration for all the photos in your project, click **Applies to all stills** (□ changes to ☑).

⑤ Click **Done**.

Add a Music Track

You can enhance the audio component of your movie by adding one or more songs that play in the background.

To get the best audio experience, you can adjust various sound properties, including the volume of the music clip, the volume of the video clip, and how the song clip fades in and out.

Add a Music Track

① Click the **Music and Sound Effects browser** button (🎵).

● iMovie displays the available audio files.

② Click the folder, category, or playlist that contains the track you want to add.

③ Use your mouse (▶) to click and drag the song and drop it on a video clip.

● iMovie adds the song to the movie.

Note: iMovie treats the song like a clip, which means you can trim the song as needed, as described earlier in the "Trim a Clip" section.

④ Double-click the music clip.

iMovie displays the Inspector.

5 Click the **Audio** tab.

6 Use the **Volume** slider to adjust the volume of the music clip.

7 If you want to reduce the video clip volume, click **Ducking** (☐ changes to ☑) and then click and drag the slider.

8 To adjust the fade-in time, click **Fade In: Manual** (○ changes to ⊙) and then click and drag the slider.

9 To adjust the fade-out time, click **Fade Out: Manual** (○ changes to ⊙) and then click and drag the slider.

10 Click **Done**.

TIP

When I add a video clip before the music clip, the music does not play with the new video clip. How can I work around this?

You need to add your song as a background track instead of a clip. Follow these steps:

1 Click 🎵.

2 Use your mouse (▲) to click and drag a song.

3 Drop the song on the project background, not on a clip or between two clips.

● The background turns green when you have the song positioned correctly.

Note: You can add multiple background tracks, and then click **Edit** and **Arrange Music Tracks** to reorder them. To pin a music track to a particular video clip, click and drag the song title to the beginning of the video clip.

Record a Voiceover

You can augment the audio portion of your movie by recording a voiceover. A voiceover is useful for explaining a video clip, introducing the movie, or giving the viewer background information about the movie.

To record a voiceover, your Mac must either have a built-in microphone or an external microphone connected either via the audio jack, USB port, or Bluetooth.

Record a Voiceover

1 If your Mac does not have a built-in microphone, attach a microphone.

Note: *You may need to configure the microphone as the sound input device. Click **System Preferences** ( ), click **Sound**, click **Input**, and then click your microphone.*

2 Click the **Voiceover** button ( ).

The Voiceover dialog appears.

3 Click the spot in the movie at which you want the voiceover to begin.

iMovie counts down and then begins the recording.

④ Speak your voiceover text into the microphone.

● The progress of the recording appears here.

⑤ When you are finished, click **Recording**.

● iMovie adds the voiceover to the clip.

⑥ Click **Close** (☒).

You can double-click the voiceover to adjust the audio, as described in the previous section.

Is there a way to tell if my voice is too loud or too soft?
Yes, you can use the controls in the Voiceover dialog. You check your voice level by talking into the microphone and then watching the Left and Right volume meters:

● If you see no green bars or just a few green bars, your voice level is too low.

● If you see yellow or red bars, your voice level is too high.

Use the Input Volume slider to adjust the voice level up or down, as needed.

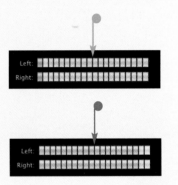

Add Titles and Credits

You can get your movie off to a proper start by adding a title and a subtitle. iMovie offers a number of title styles that you can choose from. You can also enhance your movie with scrolling credits at the end.

Add Titles and Credits

① Click the **Titles browser** button (T).

● iMovie displays the available title types.

② Use your mouse (k) to click and drag a title and drop it where you want the titles to appear.

Note: To see just the titles, drop the title thumbnail at the beginning of the movie or between two clips. To superimpose the titles on a video clip, drop the title thumbnail on the clip.

● If you want to add credits, click and drag the **Scrolling Credits** thumbnail and drop it at the end of the movie.

● iMovie adds a clip for the title.

③ Replace this text with the movie title.

④ Replace this text with the movie subtitle.

⑤ Click **Done**.

Note: *iMovie treats the title like a clip, which means you can lengthen or shorten the title duration by clicking and dragging the beginning or end, as described earlier in the "Trim a Clip" section.*

TIP

How do I change the font of the titles?
The Text menu offers several font-related commands, including Bold, Italic, Bigger, and Smaller. You can also click the **Show Fonts** command to display the Fonts dialog. To work with iMovie's predefined fonts, click **iMovie Font Panel** and then click a typeface, font color, and type size; click **Done** to close the dialog (●).

Play the Movie

While you are building your iMovie project, it is a good idea to occasionally play some or all of the movie to make sure the video and audio are working properly and the transitions appear when you want them to.

Play the Movie

Play from the Beginning

1 Click **View**.

2 Click **Play from Beginning**.

Note: *You can also press* ◯ *or click the **Play Project from beginning** button* (▶).

Play from a Specific Location

1 Position the mouse ▸ over the spot where you want to start playing the movie.

2 Press `Spacebar`.

Play a Selection

① Select the video clips you want to play.

Note: *See the Tip below to learn how to select multiple video clips.*

② Click **View**.

③ Click **Play Selection**.

Note: *You can also press /.*

 TIPS

How do I select multiple video clips?

To select multiple video clips, press and hold ⌘ and then click anywhere inside each clip you want to select. If you select a clip by accident, ⌘+click it again to deselect it.

If you want to skip just a few clips, first press ⌘ + A to select all the clips, then press and hold ⌘ and click the clips you do not want in the selection.

Can I enlarge the size of the playback pane?

Yes, you can play your movie in full-screen mode. To do this, click **View** and then click **Play full-screen**. You can also press ⌘ + G or click the **Play Project full screen** button (▶).

Create a DVD of Your Movie

When your movie project is complete, you can burn it to a recordable DVD disc for playback on your Mac or on your home or portable DVD player.

You can customize your DVD by choosing a theme, modifying the menu title, and adding a photo to the theme's drop zone, if it has one.

1 Insert a blank DVD in your Mac's DVD drive.

If your Mac asks what action you want to take with the blank DVD, click **Ignore**.

2 Click **Share**.

3 Click **iDVD**.

iMovie creates your movie.

Note: *It may take a while for iMovie to create the movie, depending on the movie length and the number of transitions and other elements you added.*

The iDVD window appears with your movie already added to the project.

4 Double-click the menu title.

5 Use the pop-up menus to set the title font.

6 Type a new title and then press **Return**.

7 Click **Themes**.

8 Click the theme you want to use.

Note: *If iDVD displays the Change Project Aspect Ratio dialog, click **Change**.*

⑨ Click **File**.

⑩ Click **Burn DVD**.

● You can also click the **Burn** button (⬛) or press ⌘ + R.

iDVD burns the movie to the DVD.

⑪ Click **Done**.

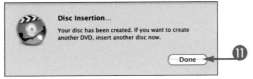

 TIPS

How do I publish my movie to YouTube?

First, you need a YouTube account. If you do not have a YouTube account, go to the YouTube Web site (www.youtube.com), click the **Sign Up** link, and follow the instructions. In iMovie, click **Share** and then click **YouTube**. Click **Add**, type your YouTube user name, and then click **Done**. Type your YouTube password, choose the size to publish (Mobile or Medium), click **Next**, and then click **Publish**.

How do I publish my movie to MobileMe?

If you have a MobileMe account, click **System Preferences** (⬛), click **MobileMe**, and then click **Sign In**. In iMovie, click **Share** and then click **MobileMe**. Click the sizes you want to publish (Tiny, Mobile, Medium, or Large), and then click **Publish**.

Surfing the World Wide Web

If your Mac is connected to the Internet, either directly or through a network connection, you can use the Safari Web browser application to navigate — or *surf* — the sites of the World Wide Web. This chapter shows you how to navigate from site to site and how to make surfing the Web easier.

Open and Close Safari

Your Mac includes the Safari application to enable you to surf Web sites when your Mac is connected to the Internet. You can also use Safari to save your favorite sites and navigate your surfing history.

Open and Close Safari

Open Safari

1 Click **Finder** (🖥) in the Dock.

2 Click **Applications**.

3 Double-click **Safari**.

The Safari window appears.

Note: *The initial Web page you see depends on how your version of Safari has been configured. In most cases, you see either the Apple.com Start page or the Top Sites page.*

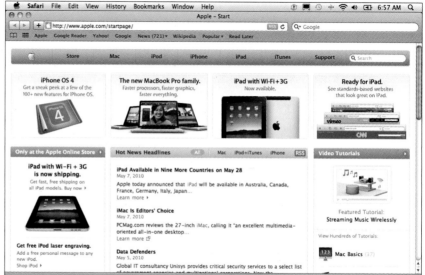

Close Safari

① Click **Safari**.

② Click **Quit Safari**.

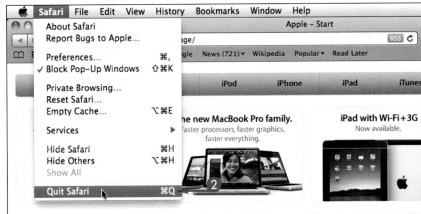

Are there faster methods I can use to open Safari?

The fastest way to start Safari is to click the **Safari** icon (🧭) in the Dock. If you have used Safari recently, another reasonably fast method is to click 🍎, click **Recent Items**, and then click **Safari**.

Are there faster methods I can use to close Safari?

Probably the fastest method you can use to quit Safari is to `Control` + click or right-click 🧭 and then click **Quit**. If your hands are closer to the keyboard than to the mouse, you can quit Safari by pressing ⌘ + Q.

Almost all Web pages include links to other pages that contain information related to something in the current page, and you can use these links to navigate to other Web pages. When you select a link, your Web browser loads the other page.

It is not always obvious which words, phrases, or images are links. Often, the only way to tell for sure is to position the mouse (⬉) over the text or image; if the ⬉ changes to 👆, you know you are dealing with a link.

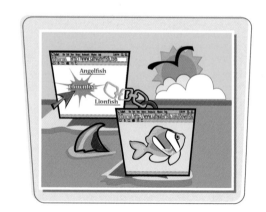

Select a Link

① Position ⬉ over the link
(⬉ changes to 👆).

● The status bar shows the address of the linked page.

② Click the text or image.

Note: The address shown in the status bar when you point at a link may be different from the one shown when the page is downloading. This occurs when the Web site "redirects" the link.

*Note: If you do not see the status bar, click **View** then click **Show Status Bar**.*

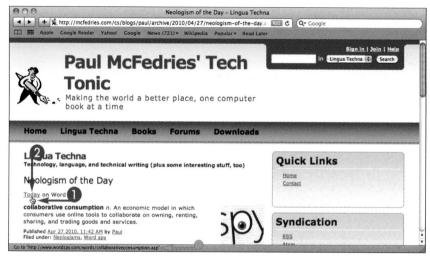

The linked Web page appears.

● The status bar shows the current download status.

● The Web page title and address change once the linked page begins loading.

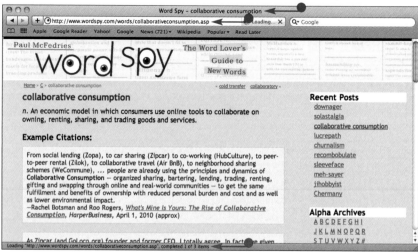

Enter a Web Page Address

If you know the address of a specific Web page, you can type it into the Web browser and the program displays the page.

Enter a Web Page Address

1. Click inside the address bar.

2. Press **Del** to delete the existing address.

3. Type the address of the Web page you want to visit.

4. Press **Return**.

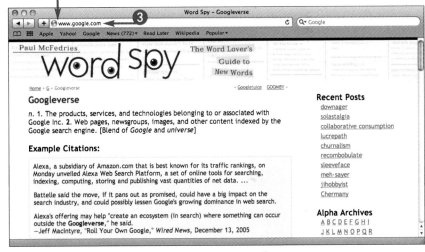

The Web page appears.

● The Web page title changes once the page begins loading.

Open a Web Page in a Tab

You can make it easier to work with multiple Web pages and sites simultaneously by opening each page in its own tab.

You can open as many pages as you want in their own tabs. This is convenient because all the pages appear within a single Safari window.

Open a Web Page in a Tab

Open a Link in a New Tab

1. **Control** +click or right-click the link you want to open.

2. Click **Open Link in New Tab**.

● A new tab appears with the page title.

3. Click the tab to display the page.

Create a New Tab

1 Click **File**.

2 Click **New Tab**.

● Safari creates a new tab.

● Safari displays the Top Sites screen, which shows the dozen sites that you have visited most often.

● If you see the page you want, click it and skip the rest of these steps.

3 Type the address of the page you want to load into the new tab.

4 Press [Return].

● Safari displays the page in the tab.

TIP

Are there any shortcuts I can use to open Web pages in tabs?

Yes. Here are some useful keyboard techniques:

● Press and hold ⌘ and click a link to open the page in a tab.

● Press and hold ⌘ + [Shift] and click a link to open the page in a tab and display the tab.

● Type an address and then press ⌘ + [Return] to open the page in a new tab.

● Type an address and then press [Shift] + ⌘ + [Return] to open the page in a new foreground tab.

● Press [Shift] + ⌘ + [ ]] or [Shift] + ⌘ + [[ ] to cycle through the tabs.

● Press ⌘ + [W] to close the current tab.

● Press [Option] and click 🗙 to close every tab but the one you clicked.

Navigate Web Pages

After you have visited several pages, you can return to a page you visited earlier. Instead of retyping the address or looking for the link, Safari gives you some easier methods.

When you navigate Web pages, you can go back to a page you have visited in the current browser session. After you have done that, you can also reverse course and go forward through the pages again.

Navigate Web Pages

Go Back One Page

1 Click the **Previous Page** icon (◀).

The previous page you visited appears.

Go Back Several Pages

1 Click and hold down ▶ on ◀.

A list of the pages you have visited appears.

2 Click the page you want to revisit.

The page appears.

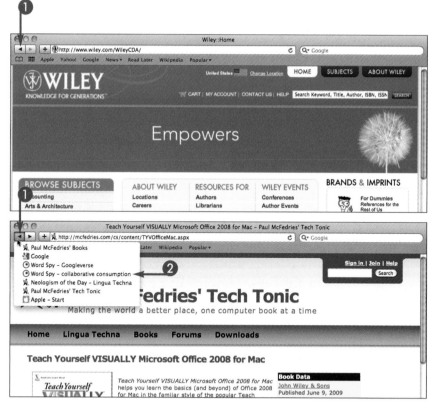

Go Forward One Page

1 Click the **Next Page** icon (▶).

The next page you visited appears.

Note: *If you are at the last page viewed up to that point, ▶ is not active.*

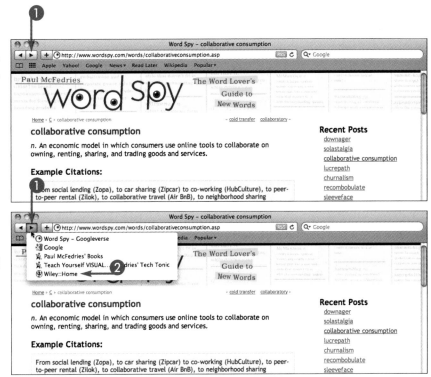

Go Forward Several Pages

1 Click and hold down ▶ on ▶.

A list of the pages you have visited appears.

2 Click the page you want to revisit.

The page appears.

Are there any shortcuts I can use to navigate Web pages?
Yes, there are a few useful keyboard shortcuts you can use:

- Press ⌘ + [to go back one page.
- Press ⌘ +] to go forward one page.
- Press Shift + ⌘ + H to return to the Safari home page (the first page you see when you open Safari).

Navigate with the History List

The Previous Page and Next Page buttons (◄ and ►) enable you to navigate pages only in the current browser session. To redisplay sites that you have visited in the past few days or weeks, you need to use the History list.

If you visit sensitive places such as an Internet banking site or your corporate site, you can increase security by clearing the History list so that other people cannot see where you have been.

Navigate with the History List

Load a Page from the History List

1 Click **History**.

2 Click the date when you visited the page.

A submenu of pages that you visited during that day appears.

3 Click the page you want to revisit.

● The page appears.

Clear the History List

1 Click **History**.

2 Click **Clear History**.

Safari deletes all the pages from the History list.

TIP

Can I control the length of time that Safari keeps track of the pages I visit?

Yes, by following these steps:

1 In the menu bar, click **Safari**.

2 Click **Preferences**.

3 Click **General**.

4 In the Remove history items pop-up menu, click 📷 and then click the amount of time you want Safari to track your history.

5 Click 📷.

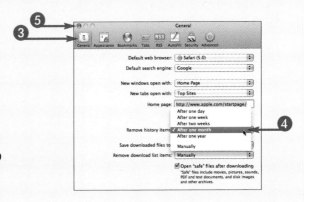

Change Your Home Page

Your home page is the Web page that appears when you first start Safari. The default home page is usually the Apple.com Start page, but you can change that to any other page you want, or even to an empty page.

Safari also comes with a command that enables you to view the home page at any time during your browsing session.

Change the Home Page

1. Display the Web page that you want to use as your home page.

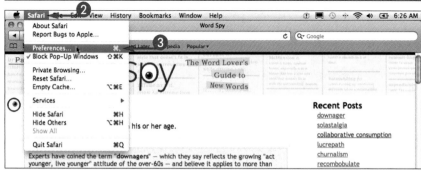

2. Click **Safari**.
3. Click **Preferences**.

④ Click **General**.

⑤ Click **Set to Current Page**.

● Safari inserts the address of the current page in the Home page text box.

Note: If your Mac is not currently connected to the Internet, you can also type the new home page address manually using the Home page text box.

⑥ Click 🔘.

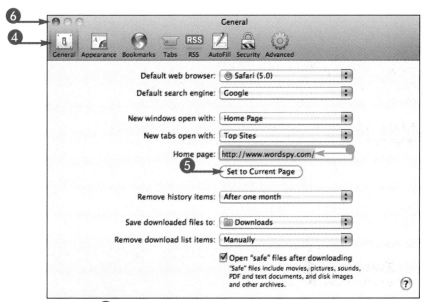

View the Home Page

① Click **History**.

② Click **Home**.

Note: You can also display the home page by pressing Shift + ⌘ + H.

Safari displays the home page.

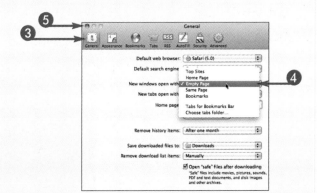

TIP

Can I get Safari to open a new window without displaying the home page?

Yes, by following these steps:

① In the menu bar, click **Safari**.

② Click **Preferences**.

③ Click **General**.

④ In the New windows open with pop-up menu, click 🔽 and then click **Empty Page**.

⑤ Click 🔘.

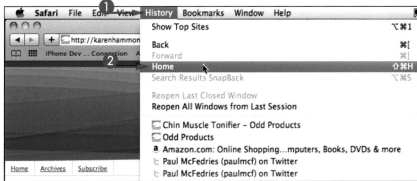

Bookmark Web Pages

If you have Web pages that you visit frequently, you can save yourself time by storing those pages as bookmarks within Safari. This enables you to display the pages with just a couple of mouse clicks.

In Safari, the Bookmarks bar appears just below the address bar. You can put your favorite sites on the Bookmarks bar for easy access.

Bookmark a Web Page

① Display the Web page you want to save as a bookmark.

② Click **Bookmarks**.

③ Click **Add Bookmark**.

● You can also run the Add Bookmark command by clicking **Add a bookmark** ([+]).

The Add Bookmark dialog appears.

Note: *You can also display the Add Bookmark dialog by pressing* ⌘ + D .

④ Edit the page name, as necessary.

⑤ Click ▤ and then click the location where you want to store the bookmark.

⑥ Click **Add**.

Safari adds a bookmark for the page.

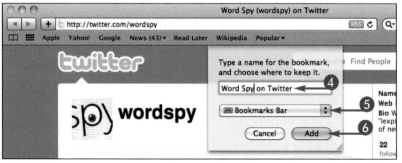

Display a Bookmarked Web Page

1 Click the bookmark name in the Bookmarks bar.

● If you added the bookmark to a folder, click the folder and then click the page name.

● If you added the bookmark to the Bookmarks menu, click **Bookmarks** and then click the page name.

The Web page appears.

TIPS

I use my Bookmarks bar a lot. Is there an easier way to display these pages?

Yes. Safari automatically assigns keyboard shortcuts to the first nine bookmarks, counting from left to right and not including folders. For example, you display the leftmost bookmark by pressing ⌘+1. Moving to the right, the shortcuts are ⌘+2, ⌘+3, and so on.

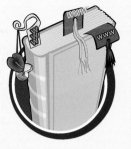

How do I delete a bookmark?

If the site is on the Bookmarks bar, Control +click or right-click the bookmark and then click **Delete**, or hold down ⌘ and drag it off the bar. For all other bookmarks, click 🔖 to display the Bookmarks window. Locate the bookmark you want to remove, Control +click or right-click the bookmark, and then click **Delete**. You can also click the bookmark and then press Del.

If you need information on a specific topic, Safari has a built-in feature that enables you to quickly search the Web for sites that have the information you require.

The Web has a number of sites called *search engines* that enable you to find what you are looking for. By default, Safari uses the Google search site (www.google.com).

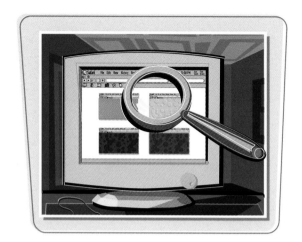

1 Click in the search box.

2 Type a word, phrase, or question that represents the information you want to find.

3 Press Return.

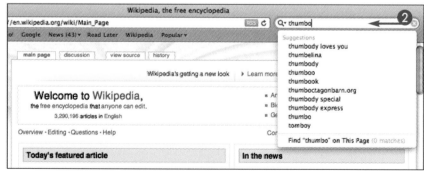

● A list of pages that match your search text appears.

④ Click a Web page.

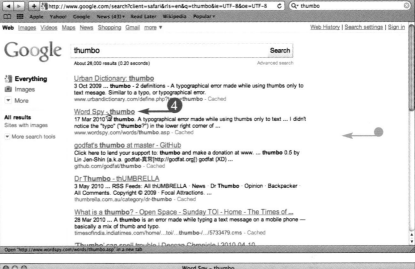

The page appears.

Is there an easy way that I can rerun a recent search?

Yes, Safari maintains a list of the last few searches you ran. Follow these steps to quickly rerun one of those searches:

❶ In the search box, click the **See your recent searches** icon ( ).

❷ Click the search you want to rerun.

● In many cases you can also click the **Snapback** icon ( ) to rerun the most recent search.

Safari sends the search text to Google again.

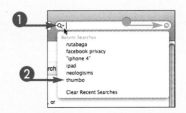

Download a File

Some Web sites make files available for you to open on your Mac. To use these files, you can download them to your Mac using Safari.

To use a file from a Web site, you must have an application designed to work with that particular file type. For example, if the file is an Excel workbook, you need either Excel for the Mac or a compatible program.

Download a File

1 Navigate to the page that contains the link to the file.

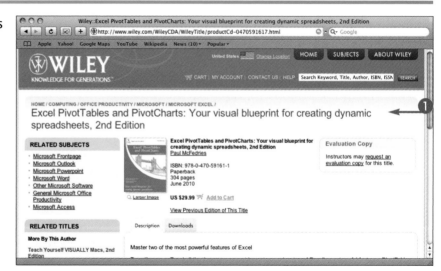

2 Click the link to the file.

Safari downloads the file to your Mac.

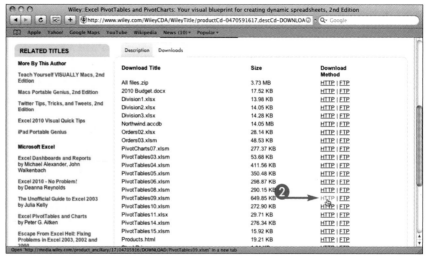

- The Downloads window shows the progress of the download.

③ When the download is complete, **Control** +click or right-click the file.

- You can also double-click the icon to the left of the file.

④ Click **Open**.

The file opens in the corresponding application.

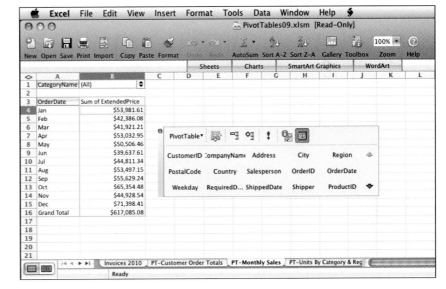

TIP

How do I remove items from my Downloads window?

① In Safari, click **Window**.

② Click **Downloads**.

You can also display the Downloads window by pressing **Option** + **⌘** + **L**.

③ **Control** +click or right-click the downloaded file to want to remove.

④ Click **Remove From List**.

- If you want to delete the downloaded file itself, click **Show in Finder** (🔍) and then delete the file from the Downloads folder.

- If you want to remove all the items in the Downloads window, click **Clear**.

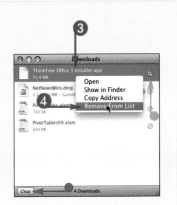

Communicating via E-Mail and Chat

You can use the Apple Mail application to send e-mail to and read e-mail from friends, family, colleagues, and even total strangers almost anywhere in the world. You can also use the iChat application to exchange instant messages. This chapter shows you how to perform these and many more communications tasks.

Open and Close Mail

Mac OS X includes the Apple Mail application to enable you to use an e-mail account to exchange and manage e-mail messages. Before you can send or receive e-mail messages, you must know how to start the Mail application.

Open Mail

① Click **Finder** ( ) in the Dock.

② Click **Applications**.

③ Double-click the **Mail** icon ( ).

Note: If the Welcome to Mail dialog appears, see the next section to learn how to set up your first e-mail account in Mail.

The Mail window appears.

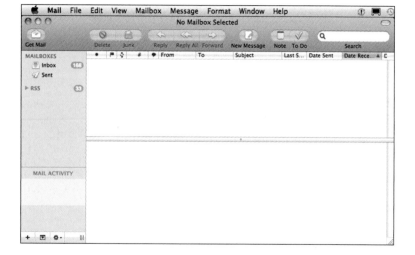

Close Mail

1 Click **Mail**.

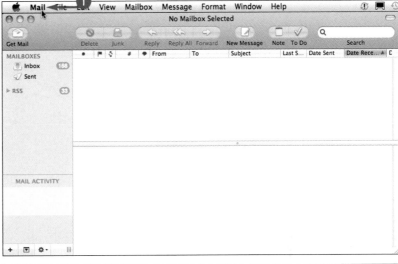

2 Click **Quit Mail**.

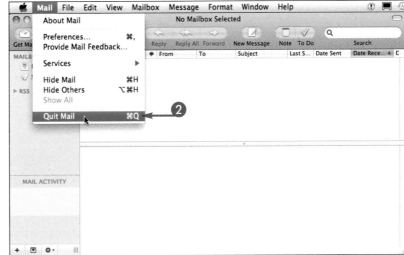

TIPS

Are there faster methods I can use to open Mail?

The fastest way to start Mail is to click the Mail icon (📮) in the Dock. If you have used Mail recently, another reasonably fast method is to click 🍎, click **Recent Items**, and then click **Mail**.

Are there faster methods I can use to close Mail?

Probably the fastest method you can use to quit Mail is to Control +click or right-click 📮 in the Dock and then click **Quit**. If your hands are closer to the keyboard than to the mouse, you can quit Mail by pressing ⌘ + Q.

Add an E-Mail Account

Before you can send an e-mail message, you must add your e-mail account to the Mail application. This also enables you to use Mail to retrieve the messages that others have sent to your account.

Your e-mail account is usually a POP (Post Office Protocol) account supplied by your Internet service provider, which should have supplied you with the POP account details. You can also set up Mail with your MobileMe account, if you have one.

Get Started Adding an Account

1 Click **File**.

2 Click **Add Account**.

Note: *If you are just starting Mail and the Welcome to Mail dialog is on-screen, you can skip Steps 1 and 2.*

The Add Account dialog appears. If you are starting Mail for the first time, the Welcome to Mail dialog is identical.

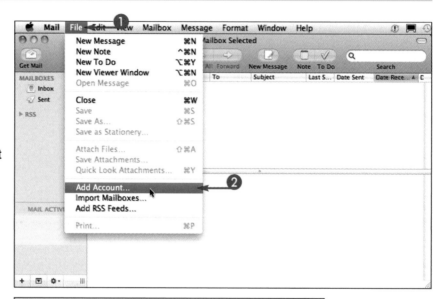

Add a MobileMe Account

1 Type your name.

2 Type your MobileMe account address.

3 Type your MobileMe account password.

4 Click **Create**.

Mail adds your MobileMe account.

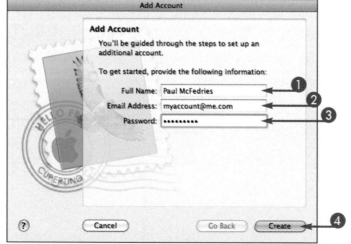

Add a POP Account

① Type your name.

② Type your POP account address.

③ Type your POP account password. Click **Continue**.

④ Click 🔹 and then click **POP**.

⑤ Describe the account.

⑥ Type the address of the account's incoming mail server.

Note: The incoming mail server may be called the POP or POPD server.

⑦ Edit the User Name text as required. Click **Continue**.

⑧ Type a Description of the outgoing mail server.

⑨ Type the address of the Outgoing Mail Server.

Note: The incoming mail server is also sometimes called the SMTP server.

● If your ISP requires authentication, click **Use Authentication** (☐ changes to ☑).

⑩ Click **Continue**. Click **Continue** again. Click **Create**.

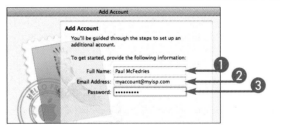

TIP

My e-mail account requires me to use a nonstandard outgoing mail port. How do I set this up?

① In the menu bar, click **Mail**.

② Click **Preferences**.

③ Click **Accounts**.

④ In the Outgoing Mail Server (SMTP) list, click 🔹 and then click **Edit SMTP Server List**.

⑤ Click the outgoing mail server.

⑥ Click **Advanced**.

⑦ Click **Use custom port** (○ changes to ◉).

⑧ Type the nonstandard port number.

⑨ Click **OK**.

⑩ Click 🔲.

⑪ Click **Save**.

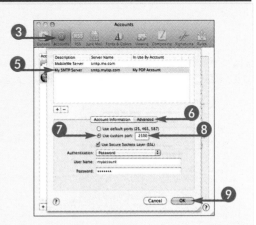

Send an E-Mail Message

If you know the e-mail address of a person or organization, you can send an e-mail message to that address. In most cases, the message is delivered within a few minutes.

If you do not know any e-mail addresses, or if at first you prefer to just practice sending messages, you can send messages to your own e-mail address.

Send an E-Mail Message

① Click **New Message**.

Note: You can also start a new message by pressing ⌘ + N .

A message window appears.

② Use the To field to type the e-mail address of the person to whom you are sending the message.

③ To send a copy of the message to another person, use the Cc field to type that person's e-mail address.

Note: You can add multiple e-mail addresses in both the To line and the Cc line. Separate each address with a comma (,).

④ Use the Subject field to type a title or short description for the message.

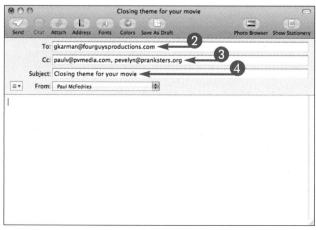

5 Type the message.

● To change the message font, you can click **Fonts** to display the Font dialog.

● To change the text colors, you can click **Colors** to display the Color Picker.

● To change the overall look of the message, click **Show Stationery** and then click a theme.

Note: *Many people use e-mail programs that cannot process text formatting. Unless you are sure your recipient's program supports formatting, it is best to send plain-text messages. To do this, click **Format** and then click **Make Plain Text**.*

6 Click **Send**.

Mail sends your message.

Note: *Mail stores a copy of your message in the Sent folder.*

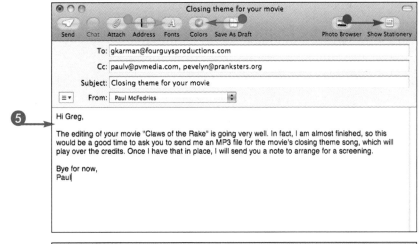

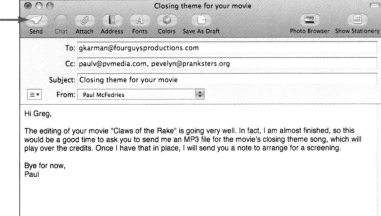

I have a large number of messages to compose. Do I have to be online to do this?

No, composing all the messages while you are offline is possible. Follow these steps:

1 In Mail, click **Mailbox** and then click **Take All Accounts Offline**.

2 Compose and send the message. Each time you click **Send**, your message is stored temporarily in the Outbox folder.

3 When you are done, connect to the Internet.

4 In Mail, click **Mailbox** and then click **Take All Accounts Online**.

After a few moments, Mail automatically sends all the messages sitting in the Outbox folder.

Add a File Attachment

If you have a memo, photo, or other document that you want to send to another person, you can attach the document to an e-mail message. The other person can then open the document after he or she receives your message.

1 Click **New Message**.

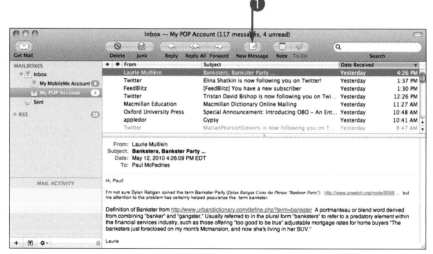

A message window appears.

2 Click **Attach** (📎).

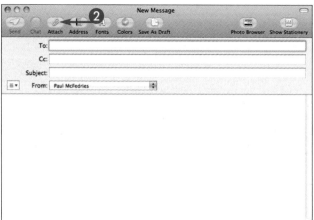

A file selection dialog appears.

③ Click the file you want to attach.

④ Click **Choose File**.

● Mail attaches the file to the message.

Note: *Another way to attach a file to a message is to click and drag the file from Finder and drop it inside the message.*

⑤ Repeat Steps **2** to **4** to attach additional files to the message.

⑥ Fill in the rest of the fields and then send your message as described in the previous section.

Is there a limit to the number of files I can attach to a message?

The number of files you can attach to the message has no practical limit. However, you should be careful with the total *size* of the files you send. If you or the recipient has a slow Internet connection, sending or receiving the message can take an extremely long time. Also, many ISPs place a limit on the size of a message's attachments, which is usually between 2MB and 5MB. In general, use e-mail to send only a few small files at a time.

Add a Signature

In an e-mail message, a *signature* is a small amount of text that appears at the bottom of the message. Instead of typing this information manually in each message, you can create the signature once and then have Mail automatically add the signature to any message you send.

Signatures usually contain personal contact information, such as your phone numbers, business address, and e-mail and Web site addresses. Some people supplement their signatures with wise or witty quotations.

Add a Signature

Create a Signature

① Click **Mail**.

② Click **Preferences**.

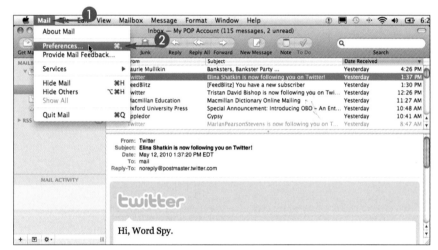

The Mail preferences appear.

③ Click **Signatures**.

④ Click the account for which you want to use the signature.

⑤ Click **Create a signature** (⊞).

Mail adds a new signature.

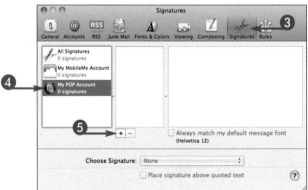

6 Type a name for the signature.

7 Type the signature text.

8 Repeat Steps 4 to 7 to add other signatures, if required.

Note: You can add as many signatures as you want. For example, you may want to have one signature for business use and another for personal use.

9 Click .

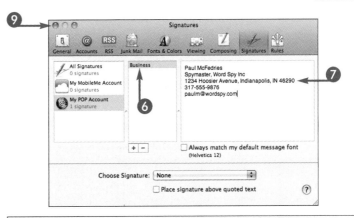

Insert the Signature

1 Click **New Message** to start a new message.

2 In the message text area, move the insertion point to the location where you want the signature to appear.

3 Click and then click the signature you want to insert.

● The signature appears in the message.

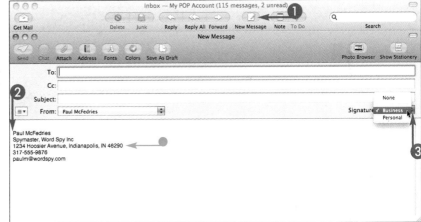

Can Mail add my signature automatically?

1 Follow Steps 1 to 4 to display the signature preferences and choose an account.

2 Click and then click the signature you want to insert automatically into each message.

3 Click **Place signature above quoted text** (changes to).

If you prefer that your signature appear at the very bottom of your replies and forwards, turn off the **Place signature above quoted text** check box (changes to).

4 Click .

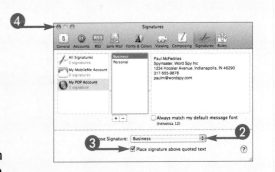

Receive and Read E-Mail Messages

A message sent to you by another person is stored on your ISP's e-mail server computer. You must connect to the ISP's computer to retrieve and read the message. As you see in this section, Mail does most of the work for you automatically.

Mail automatically checks for new messages when you start the program, and then checks for more messages every 5 minutes while you are online.

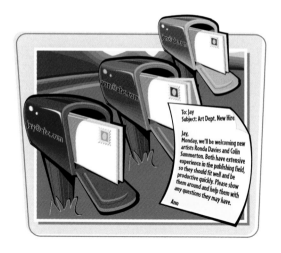

Receive and Read E-Mail Messages

Receive E-Mail Messages

1 Click **Get Mail**.

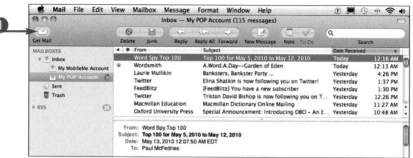

● The Mail Activity area lets you know if you have any incoming messages.

● If you have new messages, they appear in your Inbox folder with a blue dot in this column.

● The ◉ icon in the Dock shows the number of unread messages in the Inbox folder.

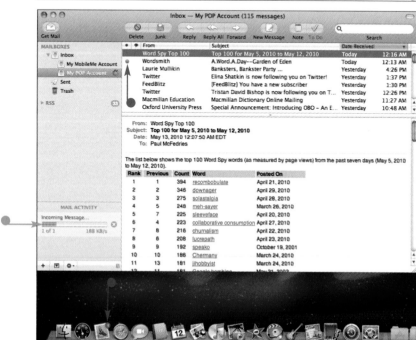

Read a Message

1 Click the message.

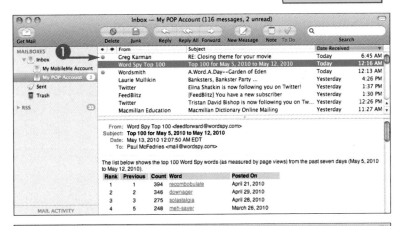

2 Read the message text in the preview pane.

Note: *If you want to open the message in its own window, double-click the message.*

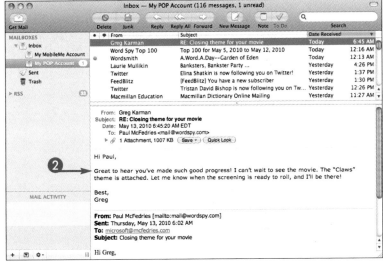

Can I change how often Mail automatically checks for messages?

Yes, by following these steps:

1 Click **Mail**.

2 Click **Preferences**.

The Mail preferences appear.

3 Click the **General** tab.

4 In the Check for new messages pop-up menu, click
⬦ and then click the time interval that you want
Mail to use when checking for new messages
automatically.

● If you do not want Mail to check for messages
automatically, click **Manually** instead.

5 Click 🔲.

When a message you receive requires some kind of response — whether it is answering a question, supplying information, or providing comments or criticisms — you can send a reply to the person who sent that message.

Reply to a Message

① Click the message to which you want to reply.

② Click the reply type you want to use.

Click **Reply** (⬛) to respond only to the person who sent the message.

Click **Reply All** (⬛) to respond to all the addresses in the message's From, To, and Cc lines.

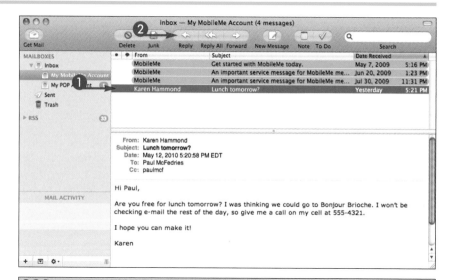

A message window appears.

● Mail automatically inserts the recipient addresses.

● Mail also inserts the subject line, preceded by Re:.

● Mail includes the original message text at the bottom of the reply.

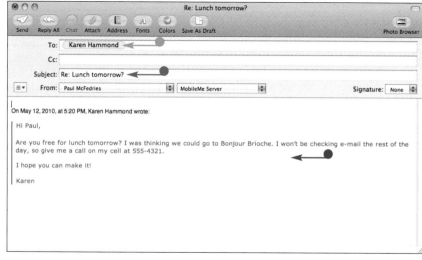

③ Edit the original message to include only the text relevant to your reply.

Note: If the original message is fairly short, you usually do not need to edit the text. However, if the original message is long, and your response deals only with part of that message, you will save the recipient time and confusion by deleting everything except the relevant portion of the text.

④ Click the area above the original message text and type your reply.

⑤ Click **Send**.

Mail sends your reply.

Note: Mail stores a copy of your reply in the Sent folder.

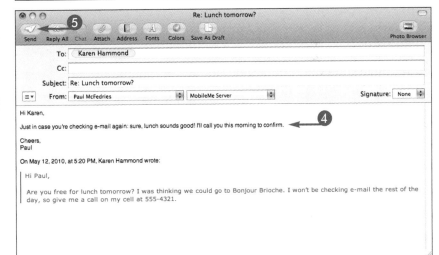

I received a message inadvertently. Is there a way that I can pass it along to the correct recipient?

Yes. Mail comes with a feature that enables you to pass along inadvertent messages to the correct recipient. Click the message that you received inadvertently, click **Message**, and then click **Redirect** (or press Shift + ⌘ + E). Type the recipient's address and then click **Send**. Replies to this message will be sent to the original sender, not to you.

How should I respond to a message that is hostile or rude?

If you receive an unpleasant message, it is best not to respond directly to the sender because that most often just encourages that person to send you more messages. A much better way to handle this situation is to return a *bounce* message that makes it appear your address is not valid. Click the message that you received, click **Message**, and then click **Bounce** (or press Shift + ⌘ + B).

Forward a Message

If a message has information that is relevant to or concerns another person, you can forward a copy of that message to the other recipient. You can also include your own comments in the forward.

① Click the message that you want to forward.

② Click **Forward** (□).

Note: You can also press Shift + ⌘ + F.

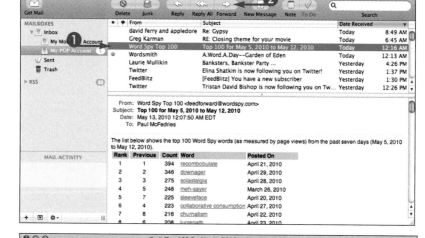

A message window appears.

● Mail inserts the subject line, preceded by Fwd:.

● The original message's addresses (To and From), date, subject, and text are included at the bottom of the forward.

③ Type the e-mail address of the person to whom you are forwarding the message.

④ To send a copy of the forward to another person, type that person's e-mail address (shown here in the Cc line).

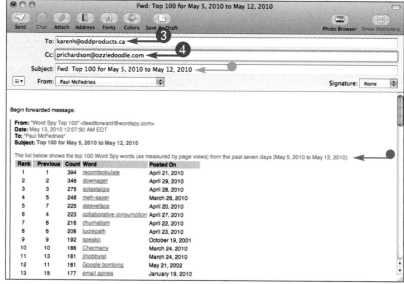

⑤ Edit the original message to include only the text relevant to your forward.

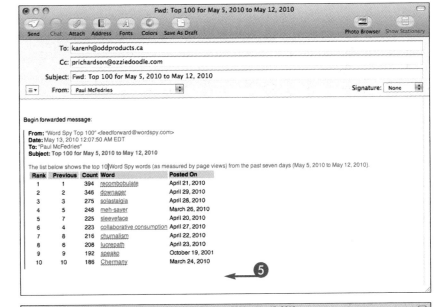

⑥ Click the area above the original message text and type your comments.

⑦ Click **Send**.

Mail sends your forward.

Note: Mail stores a copy of your forward in the Sent folder.

*Note: You can forward someone a copy of the actual message instead of just a copy of the message text. Click the message, click **Message**, and then click **Forward As Attachment**. Mail creates a new message and includes the original message as an attachment.*

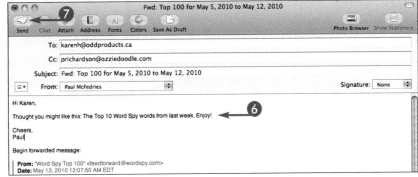

Mail always formats my replies as rich text, even when the original message is plain text. How can I fix this problem?

You can configure Mail to always reply using the same format as the original message. Follow these steps:

① Click **Mail**.

② Click **Preferences**.

The Mail preferences appear.

③ Click the **Composing** tab.

④ Click the **Use the same message format as the original message** check box (☐ changes to ☑).

⑤ Click ◉.

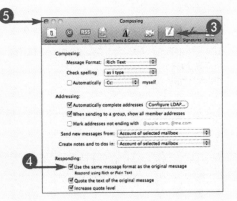

Open and Close iChat

Mac OS X includes the iChat application to enable you to exchange instant messages with other people who are online, as well as carry on audio and video chats. Before you can chat with another person, you must know how to start the iChat application.

The first time you open iChat, you must run through a short configuration process to set up your account.

Open and Close iChat

Open iChat

1. Click **Finder** (🖥️) in the Dock.
2. Click **Applications**.
3. Double-click **iChat**.

Configure Your iChat Account

The first time you open iChat, the Welcome to iChat dialog appears.

1. Click **Continue**.

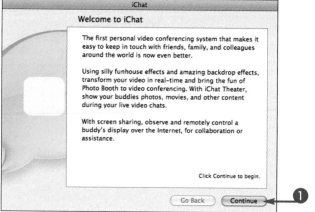

The Account Setup dialog appears.

2. In the Account Type pop-up menu, click 🔽 and then click the type of account you want to use with iChat.

3. Type the account name.

4. Type the account password.

5. Click **Continue**.

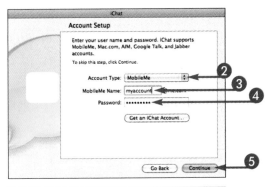

If you are using a MobileMe account, the Encrypted iChat dialog appears.

6. If you do not need to encrypt your messages for security, click **Enable iChat encryption** (☑ changes to ☐).

7. Click **Continue**.

The Conclusion dialog appears.

8. Click **Done**.

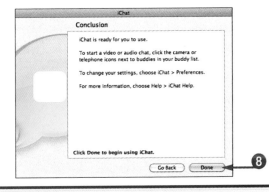

TIPS

Are there faster methods I can use to open iChat?

The fastest way to start iChat is to click the **iChat** icon (🟦) in the Dock. If you have used iChat recently, another reasonably fast method is to click 🟦, click **Recent Items**, and then click **iChat**.

How do I close iChat?

In the menu bar, click **iChat** and then click **Quit iChat**. Probably the fastest method you can use to quit iChat is to Control + click or right-click 🟦 and then click **Quit**. If your hands are closer to the keyboard than to the mouse, you can quit iChat by pressing ⌘+Q.

Add a Buddy

You send instant messages to, and receive instant messages from, the people in your *buddy list*, which is also called a *contact list*. Before you can send an instant message to a person, you must add the person to your iChat buddy list.

iChat enables you to maintain your buddy list by adding and deleting people, and it tells you the current online status of each person on the list.

Add a Buddy

① Click **Buddies**.

② Click **Add Buddy**.

Note: *You can also run the Add Buddy command by pressing* Shift *+* ⌘ *+* A .

iChat prompts you for the buddy's account information.

③ Use the Account name text box to specify your buddy's AIM screen name or MobileMe address.

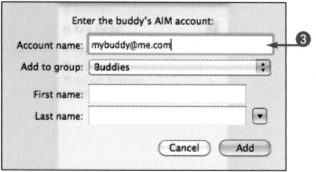

4️⃣ Use the First name text box to type your buddy's first name.

5️⃣ Use the Last name text box to type your buddy's last name.

6️⃣ Click **Add**.

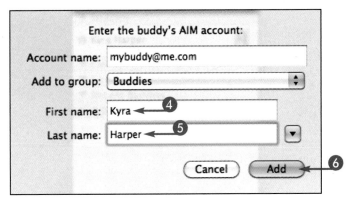

● iChat adds the person to your buddy list.

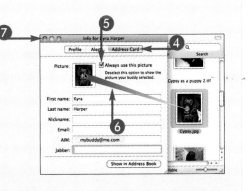

TIP

Is there a way to change the picture that iChat uses for my buddy?

Yes. By default, iChat uses whatever picture your buddy has configured for himself or herself. To display a different picture, follow these steps:

1️⃣ Click the buddy.

2️⃣ Click **Buddies**.

3️⃣ Click **Show Info**.

4️⃣ Click **Address Card**.

5️⃣ Click **Always use this picture** (☐ changes to ☑).

6️⃣ Click and drag the picture you want to use and drop it on the Picture box.

7️⃣ Click 🔲.

Start a Text Chat

In iChat, an instant messaging conversation is most often the exchange of text messages between two or more people who are online and available to chat.

An instant messaging conversation begins by one person inviting another person to exchange messages. In iChat, this means sending an initial instant message, and the recipient either accepts or rejects the invitation.

Start a Text Chat

Send an Invitation

1. In iChat's AIM Buddy List, make sure the person's status icon is green ().

Note: The ⬤ icon means that the person is available to chat; a red icon (⬤) means that the person is not available to chat.

2. Click the person you want to chat with.

3. Click **Buddies**.

4. Click **Invite to Chat**.

A chat window appears.

5. Type your invitation or opening message.

6. Press Return.

The invitation appears on the other person's computer.

Accept an Invitation

1. Click the invitation.

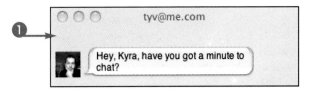

2. Type a response.

Note: *If the person who sent the message is not on your buddy list, iChat does not display the message. To see the message, you must click **Display**.*

3. Click **Accept**.

● If you cannot chat right now, click **Decline** instead.

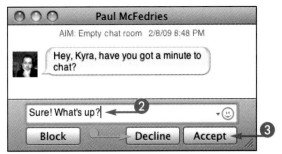

● The response appears in the chat window.

4. Repeat Steps **5** and **6** from the previous page to continue chatting.

TIPS

Are there faster methods I can use to start a text chat?

Yes. If your hand is on the mouse, use the AIM Buddy List window to click the person you want to chat with and then click the **Start a Text Chat** button (⒜). From the keyboard, you can start a text chat with the selected buddy by pressing Shift + ⌘ + M.

Can I automatically decline a person who is bothering me?

Yes. If you no longer want to receive messages from a sender who is annoying, abusive, or offensive, iChat enables you to block that sender. This means that iChat will no longer allow messages from that person to go through. When a chat alert message comes through from that person, click the message and then click **Block**. When iChat asks you to confirm, click **Block** again.

Start an Audio Chat

If you and the buddy with whom you want to converse both have a microphone attached to your computers (and speakers if they are not built in), you can converse with each other just as though you were talking over the phone. iChat comes with an *audio chat* feature that enables you to speak to another person over the Internet.

Send an Invitation

1 In iChat's AIM Buddy List, make sure the person's status icon is green (⬚).

Note: *Also make sure that the person shows the telephone icon (⬚) or the camera icon (⬚), which means the person has the equipment required for an audio chat.*

2 Click the person you want to audio chat with.

3 Click **Buddies**.

4 Click **Invite to Audio Chat**.

An audio chat window appears and iChat waits for a response to the invitation.

The invitation appears on the other person's computer.

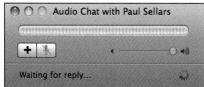

Accept an Invitation

1 Click the invitation.

2 Click **Accept**.

● If you prefer to text chat, click **Text Reply** to begin a separate text chat.

● If you cannot chat right now, click **Decline**.

iChat sets up the audio connection.

3 Use your microphone or built-in iSight camera to converse with the other person.

● You can click and drag the slider to control the chat volume.

Can I start a video chat?

Yes, if you and the contact with whom you want to converse both have a Web camera, microphone, sound card, and speakers attached to your computer, you can both see and talk to each other at the same time. iChat comes with a *video chat* feature that enables you to see each other's Web camera image and hear each other's voice. If the other person shows the camera icon (), click that person, click **Buddies**, and then click **Invite to Video Chat**.

Are there faster methods I can use to start an audio or video chat?

Yes. First, use the AIM Buddy List window to click the person you want to chat with. For an audio chat, click the **Start an Audio Chat** button (); for a video chat, click the **Start a Video Chat** button ().

Tracking Your Contacts and Events

You may find that your life is busier than ever, and the number of events you have to keep track of and tasks you have to perform seem to increase daily. Fortunately, Mac OS X comes with two applications that can help you manage your busy schedule. You use Address Book to manage your contacts, and you use iCal to enter and track events and to-do items.

Open and Close Address Book

Mac OS X includes the Address Book application to enable you to manage your contacts, whether they are colleagues, friends, or family members. Before you can add or work with contacts, you must know how to start the Address Book application.

Open and Close Address Book

Open Address Book

① Click **Finder** (⊞) in the Dock.

② Click **Applications**.

③ Double-click **Address Book**.

The Address Book window appears.

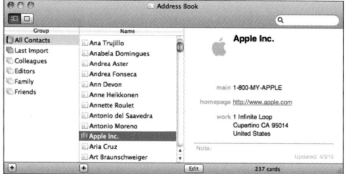

Close Address Book

① Click **Address Book**.

② Click **Quit Address Book**.

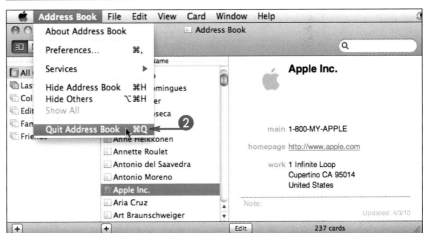

TIPS

Are there faster methods I can use to open Address Book?

The fastest way to start Address Book is to click the **Address Book** icon (▨) in the Dock. If you have used Address Book recently, another reasonably fast method is to click ▨, click **Recent Items**, and then click **Address Book**.

Are there faster methods I can use to close Address Book?

Probably the fastest method you can use to quit Address Book is to Control+click or right-click its icon (▨) and then click **Quit**. If your hands are closer to the keyboard than to the mouse, you can quit Address Book by pressing ⌘+Q.

Add a New Contact

You can store contact information for a particular person by creating a card for that person in Address Book. You can store a person's name, company name, phone numbers, address, and much more.

1 Click **File**.

2 Click **New Card**.

Note: You can also run the New Card command by pressing ⌘ + N or by clicking + in the Name column.

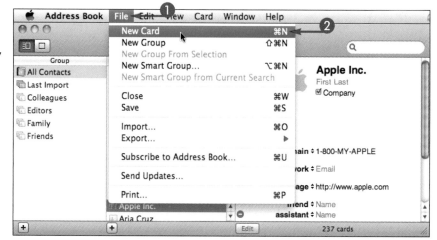

● Address Book adds a new card.

3 Use the First field to type the contact's first name.

4 Use the Last field to type the contact's last name.

5 Use the Company field to type the contact's company name.

6 If the contact is a company, click **Company** (☐ changes to ☑).

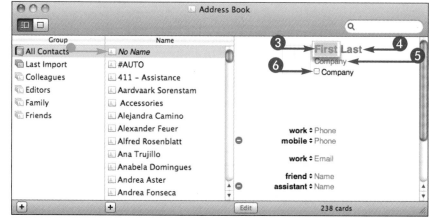

⑦ In the first Phone field, click ⬛ and then click the category you want to use.

⑧ Type the phone number.

⑨ Repeat Steps **7** and **8** to enter data in some or all of the other fields.

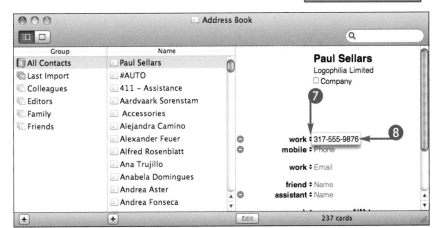

Note: See the next section to learn how to add more fields to the card.

⑩ Click **Edit**.

Address Book saves the new card.

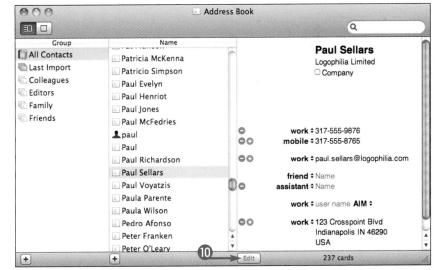

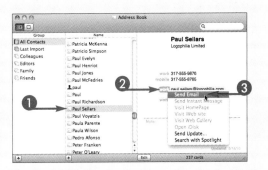

TIP

If I include a contact's e-mail address, is there a way to send that person a message without having to type the address?

Yes. You can follow these steps:

① Click the contact's card.

② Click the e-mail address category.

③ Click **Send Email**.

Apple Mail displays a new e-mail message with the contact already added in the To line.

④ Fill in the rest of the message as required.

⑤ Click **Send**.

Note: You can also start a new message in Mail: click **Address**, click the contact, and then click **To:** (or **Cc:** or **Bcc:**).

Edit a Contact

If you need to make changes to the information already in a contact's card, or if you need to add new information to a card, you can edit the card from within Address Book.

Edit a Contact

1 Click the card you want to edit.

2 Click **Edit**.

● Address Book makes the card's fields available for editing.

3 Edit the existing fields as required.

4 To add a field, click ⊕.

Note: *Address Book adds a field of the same type. For example, if you click* ⊕ *in the Phone area, Address Book adds a new Phone field.*

5 To remove a field, click ⊖.

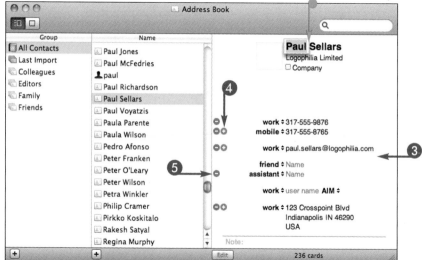

6 To add a new field type, click **Card**.

7 Click **Add Field**.

8 Click the type of field you want.

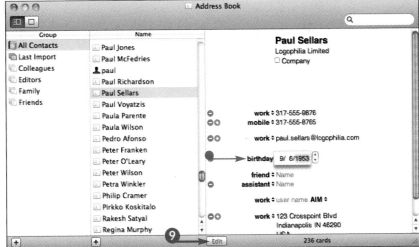

● Address Book adds the field to the card.

9 When you are done, click **Edit**.

Address Book saves the edited card.

TIP

How do I add a picture for the new contact?
Follow these steps:

1 Click the contact's card.

2 Click **Edit**.

3 Double-click the picture box.

4 Click **Choose** and choose the picture you want to use.

5 Click **Open**.

6 Click and drag the picture to the position you want.

7 Click **Set**.

8 Click **Edit**.

Create a Contact Group

You can organize your contacts into one or more groups, which is useful if you want to view just a subset of your contacts. You can create a group first and then add members, or you can select members in advance and then create the group.

Create a Contact Group

Create a Contact Group

1 Click **File**.

2 Click **New Group**.

Note: *You can also run the New Group command by pressing* Shift *+* ⌘ *+* N *or by clicking* + *below the Group column.*

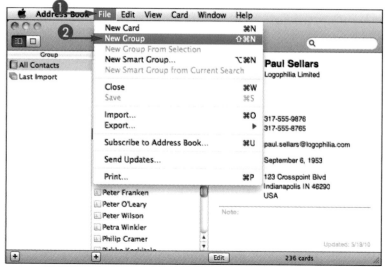

● Address Book adds a new group.

3 Type a name for the group.

4 Press Return.

5 Click **All Contacts**.

6 Click and drag a contact to the group.

Address Book adds the contact to the group.

7 Repeat Step **6** for the other contacts you want to add to the group.

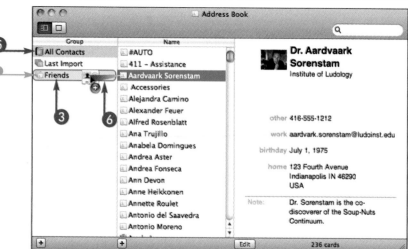

Create a Group of Selected Contacts

① Select the contacts you want to include in the new group.

Note: To select multiple contacts, press and hold ⌘ and click each card.

② Click **File**.

③ Click **New Group From Selection**.

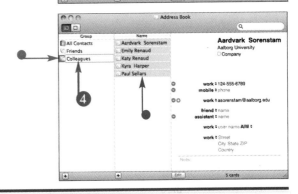

● Address Book adds a new group.

● Address Book adds the selected contacts as group members.

④ Type a name for the group.

⑤ Press **Return**.

TIPS

Can I send an e-mail message to the group?

Yes, this is one of the best reasons to create a group. Normally, sending an e-mail message to multiple contacts involves typing or selecting multiple addresses. With a group, however, you send a single message to the group, and Mail automatically sends a copy to each member. Control + click or right-click the group and then click **Send Email to "*Group*"**, where *Group* is the name of the group.

What is a smart group?

A *smart group* is a special group where each member has one or more fields in common, such as the company name, department name, city, or state. When you create the smart group, you specify one or more criteria, and then Address Book automatically adds members to the group if they meet those criteria. To create a smart group, click **File**, click **New Smart Group**, and then enter your group criteria.

Open and Close iCal

Your Mac comes with the iCal application to enable you to manage your schedule. Before you can add or work with events (appointments, meetings, all-day activities, and so on), and to-do items (tasks), you must know how to start the iCal application.

Open iCal

① Click **Finder** (🖼) in the Dock.

② Click **Applications**.

③ Double-click **iCal**.

The iCal window appears.

Close iCal

1 Click **iCal**.

2 Click **Quit iCal**.

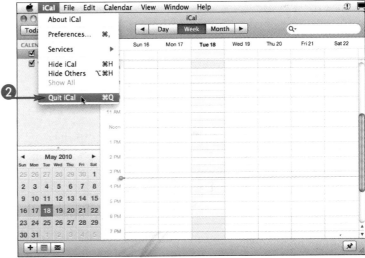

TIPS

Are there faster methods I can use to open iCal?

The fastest way to start iCal is to click the **iCal** icon (🗓) in the Dock. If you have used iCal recently, another reasonably fast method is to click 🍎, click **Recent Items**, and then click **iCal**.

Are there faster methods I can use to close iCal?

Probably the fastest method you can use to quit iCal is to Control +click or right-click its icon (🗓) and then click **Quit**. If your hands are closer to the keyboard than to the mouse, you can quit iCal by pressing ⌘ + Q.

Navigate the Calendar

Before you create an event such as an appointment or meeting, or an all-day event such as a conference or trip, you must first select the date on which the event occurs.

Use the Mini-Month

① In the mini-month, click the **Next Month** button (▶) until the month of your event appears.

● If you go too far, click the **Previous Month** button (◀) to move back to the month you want.

② Click the date.

● The date appears in the events list.

● To see just that date, click **Day** (or press ⌘+①).

● To see the date in the context of its month, click **Month** (or press ⌘+③).

● If you want to return to today's date, click **Today** (or press ⌘+Ⓣ).

Go to a Specific Date

1 Click **View**.

2 Click **Go to Date**.

Note: *You can also select the Go to Date command by pressing* Shift + ⌘ + T.

The Go to date dialog appears.

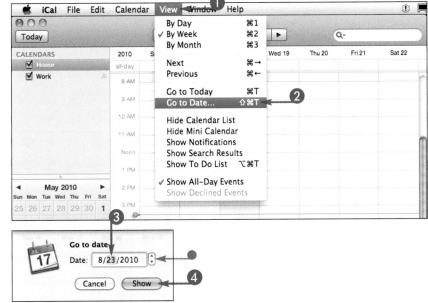

3 Use the **Date** text box to type the date you want using the format mm/dd/yyyy.

● You can also click the day, month, or year and then click ⬍ to increase or decrease the value.

4 Click **Show**.

● iCal displays the date in the events list.

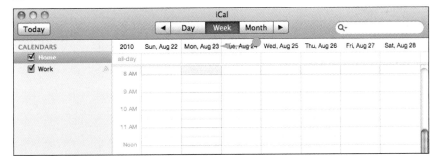

In the Week view, the week begins on Sunday. How can I change this to Monday?

iCal's default Week view has Sunday on the left and Saturday on the right. Many people prefer to display the weekend days together, with Monday on the left signaling the start of the week. To set this up, follow these steps:

1 Click **iCal** in the menu bar.

2 Click **Preferences**.

3 Click the **General** tab.

4 In the Start week on pop-up menu, click ⬍ and then click **Monday**.

5 Click ⦿.

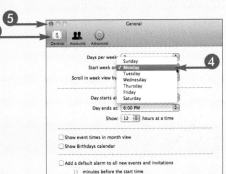

You can help organize your life by using iCal to record your events — such as appointments, meetings, phone calls, dates, and so on — on the date and time they occur.

If the event has no set time — for example, a birthday, anniversary, or multiple-day event such as a sales meeting or vacation — you can create an all-day event.

Create an Event

Create a Regular Event

1. Navigate to the date when the event occurs.

2. Click the calendar you want to use.

3. Double-click the time when the event starts.

● iCal adds a one-hour event.

Note: If the event is less than or more than an hour, you can also click and drag the mouse (➤) over the full event period.

4. Type the name of the event.

5. Press Return.

Note: Another way to create a new event is to click the start time and then press ⌘ + N.

Create an All-Day Event

① Navigate to the date when the event occurs.

② Click the calendar you want to use.

③ Double-click anywhere inside the **all-day** section.

● iCal adds a new all-day event.

④ Type the name of the event.

⑤ Press Return.

TIP

How can I specify event details such as the location and a reminder message?
Follow these steps:

① Follow the steps in this section to create an event.

② Double-click the event.

If this is the first time you have edited the event, skip to Step **4**.

③ Click **Edit**.

④ Use the location text box to type the location of the event.

⑤ Use the alarm pop-up menu to choose **Message**.

⑥ Choose the amount of time before the event that you want to receive the reminder.

⑦ Click **Done**.

iCal saves the new event configuration.

Create a
Repeating Event

If you have an activity or event that recurs at a regular interval, you can create an event and configure it to automatically repeat in iCal. You can repeat an event daily, weekly, monthly, yearly, or with a custom interval.

Create a Repeating Event

1 Follow the steps in the previous section to create an event.

2 Double-click the event.

iCal displays information for the event.

Note: You do not see this information the first time you double-click an event, in which case you can skip to Step 4.

3 Click **Edit**.

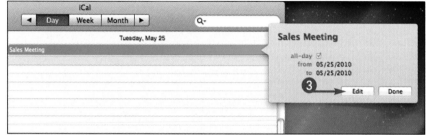

iCal opens the event for editing.

④ Beside the repeat label, click **None**.

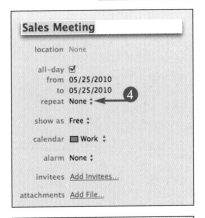

⑤ Click the interval you want to use.

● If you want to specify a custom interval such as every two weeks or the first Monday of every month, click **Custom** and configure your interval in the dialog that appears.

⑥ Click **Done**.

iCal adds the repeating events to the calendar.

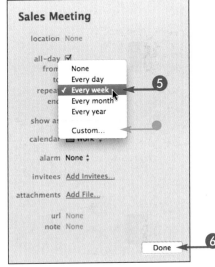

TIPS

How do I configure an event to stop after a certain number of occurrences?

Follow these steps:

① Follow Steps **1** to **5** to select a recurrence interval.

② Beside the end label, click **None** and then click **After**.

③ Type the number of occurrences you want.

④ Click **Done**.

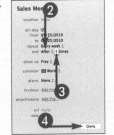

Is it possible to delete just a single occurrence out of a recurring series of events?

Yes, you can delete one occurrence from the calendar without affecting the rest of the series. Click the occurrence you want to delete, and then press Del. iCal asks whether you want to delete all the occurrences or just the selected occurrence. Click **Delete Only This Event**.

Create a To-Do Item

You can monitor to-do items — from large projects such as budgets to basic chores such as returning phone calls — by using iCal to record these tasks. You can help organize your life by giving a priority to each task.

When the to-do item is done, you should mark it as complete so you can easily tell which items remain to be done.

Create a To-Do Item

Create a To-Do Item

① Click the calendar you want to use.

② Click **File**.

③ Click **New To Do**.

Note: You can also choose the New To Do command by pressing ⌘ + K.

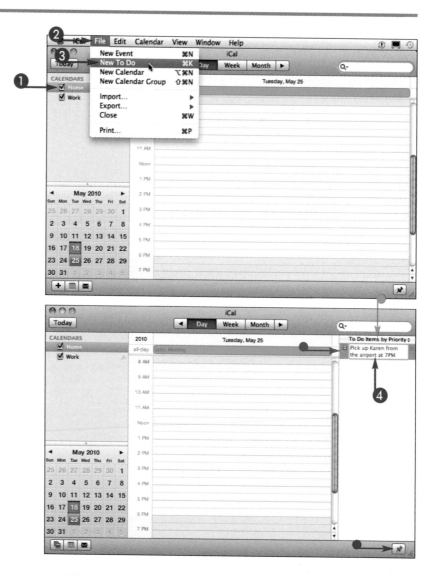

● iCal displays the To Do list.

● iCal adds a new to-do item to the list.

● You can click **View or Hide To Dos** (⬦) to toggle the To Do list on and off.

④ Type the name of the to-do item.

⑤ Press Return.

Set the Priority

1 Click the **Set Priority** icon ().

2 Click the priority you want to use.

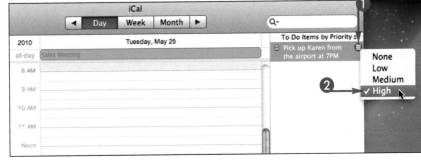

Mark a To-Do Item as Completed

1 Click the **Completed** check box (☐ changes to ☑).

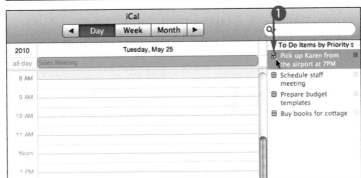

TIP

How can I specify to-do item details such as the due date and a reminder message?

Follow these steps:

1 Follow the steps in this section to create a to-do item.

2 In the To Do list, double-click the to-do item.

3 Click **due date** (☐ changes to ☑).

4 Type the date the to-do item is due.

5 Use the alarm pop-up menu to choose **Message**.

6 Choose when you want to receive the reminder.

7 Type the time you want the reminder to appear.

8 Click **Close**.

iCal saves the new to-do item configuration.

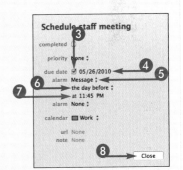

Working with Your MobileMe Account

For an annual fee, you can get a MobileMe account, which is a Web-based service that gives you e-mail, an address book, a calendar, a Web Gallery for sharing photos, and online file storage. This chapter shows you how to use all of these features of MobileMe.

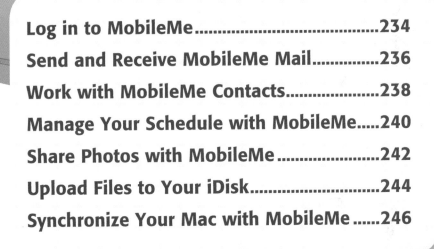

Log in to MobileMe

Before you can use any of the features associated with your MobileMe account, you must log in to the service.

Log in to MobileMe

1 In your Web browser, type **www.me.com**.

2 Press **Return**.

The MobileMe Login page appears.

3 Use the Member name text box to type your MobileMe member name.

4 Use the Password text box to type the password for your MobileMe account.

- If you want MobileMe to log you in automatically for two weeks, click **Keep me logged in for two weeks** (☐ changes to ☑).

⑤ Click **Sign In**.

Your main MobileMe account page appears.

- When you are done working with your MobileMe account, click your member name and then click **Sign Out** to log out of the account.

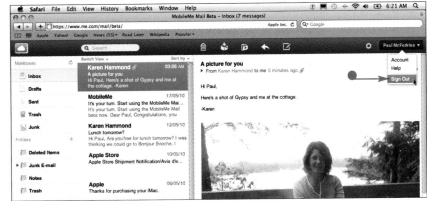

 TIPS

How do I get a MobileMe account?
Follow Steps **1** and **2**, click **Start a 60-day free trial**, and then fill in the form. You will be able to try out MobileMe free for 60 days, and then to continue you must pay a subscription fee. An Individual subscription currently costs $99 per year; a Family Pack subscription currently costs $149 per year and consists of one main account plus four subaccounts.

Can I log in from my Mac?
Yes. Click **System Preferences** (▩) in the Dock (or click ▨ and then click **System Preferences**) and then click **MobileMe**. Type your member name and password, and then click **Sign In** (●).

Send and Receive
MobileMe Mail

You can use the MobileMe Mail feature to work with your MobileMe e-mail account online. You can check for incoming messages, reply to messages, or send new messages, using either your Mac or any computer with Web access.

Display MobileMe Mail

① Log in to your MobileMe account.

Note: See the "Log in to MobileMe" section, earlier in this chapter.

② If you are using another section of MobileMe, click **Switch Apps** ([□]) and then click **Mail** ([✉]).

Get Incoming Messages

① Click **Reload** ([⟳]).

● MobileMe Mail checks for incoming messages and, if there are any, displays them in the Inbox folder.

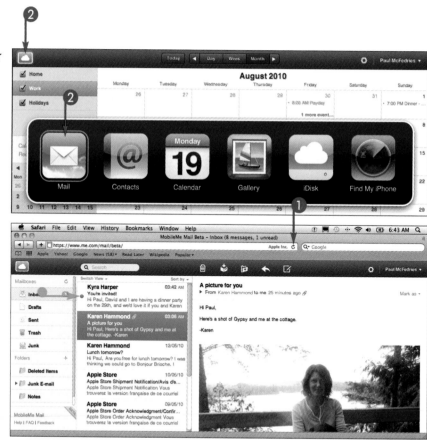

Reply to a Message

1 Click the message.

2 Click **Reply, Reply All, Forward** ().

3 Click **Reply**.

● To reply to the sender and all the recipients of the original message, click **Reply All** instead.

● To pass the message to another person, click **Forward** instead.

4 In the message window that appears (not shown), type your message and then click **Send message** (📨).

Send a New Message

1 Click **Compose new message** (📝).

2 Use the To text box to type the recipient's e-mail address.

● If you want another person to see a copy of the message, type that person's address in the Cc text box.

3 Use the Subject text box to type the subject of the message.

4 Type your message.

5 Click **Send message** (📨).

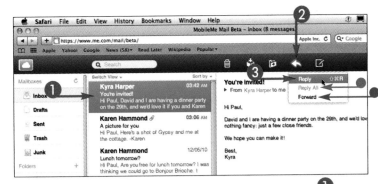

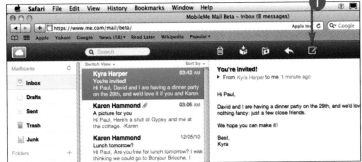

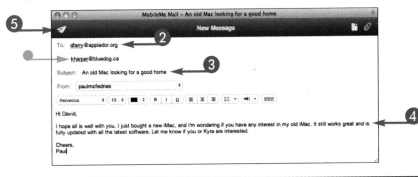

TIPS

Can I use MobileMe to send a message to a person without other recipients knowing?

Yes, you can send that person a blind courtesy copy (Bcc). To activate this feature, open MobileMe Mail, click **Actions** (⚙), click **Preferences**, and then click the **Composing** tab. Click **Show Bcc field** (☐ changes to ☑) and then click **Done**.

Can I use MobileMe Mail to send a vacation message?

1 In MobileMe Mail, click ⚙.

2 Click **Preferences**.

3 Click the **Vacation** tab.

4 Click **Automatically reply to messages when they are received** (☐ changes to ☑).

5 Type your vacation message.

6 Click **Done**.

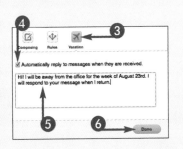

Work with MobileMe Contacts

You can use MobileMe to store information about your friends, family, colleagues, and clients. Using the Contacts application, you can store data such as the person's name, phone numbers, e-mail address, and street address.

If you already have contacts in your Mac Address Book, you can synchronize them with MobileMe. See "Synchronize Your Mac with MobileMe," later in this chapter.

Work with MobileMe Contacts

Display MobileMe Contacts

1. Log in to your MobileMe account.

Note: *See the "Log in to MobileMe" section, earlier in this chapter.*

2. Click **Switch Apps** (▢).

3. Click **Contacts** (▦).

Create a Contact

1. Click **Create a new contact** (➕).

2. Type the person's first name.

3. Type the person's last name.

4. Type the person's company's name.

5. Click ⬍ and then click a phone number category.

6. Type the phone number.

7. Click ⬍ and then click an e-mail category.

8. Type the person's e-mail address.

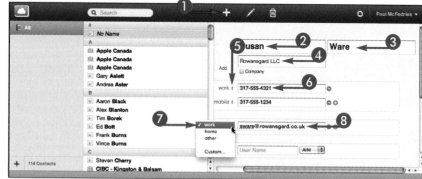

9. Click ⬦ and then click a street address category.

10. Use the text boxes in this section to type the person's street address.

11. Type a note about the person.

12. Click **Save**.

   MobileMe saves the contact.

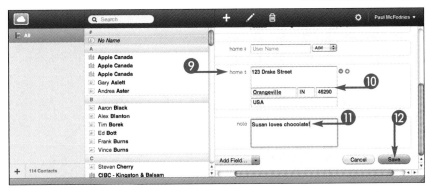

Display a Contact

1. Use the scroll bar to locate the contact.

2. Click the contact.

● MobileMe displays the contact's details.

● You can also type part of the contact's name in the Search box.

● To e-mail the contact, click the address.

● To make changes to the contact, click **Edit** (✎).

● To remove the contact, click **Delete** (🗑).

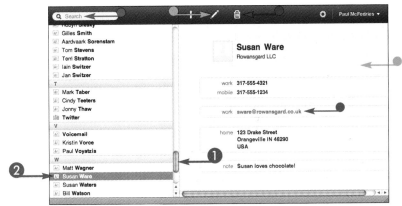

TIPS

How do I add a photo for a contact?

To add a photo to an existing contact, click the contact and then click **Edit**. Click **Add** to open the Add Photo dialog, click **Choose Photo**, click the photo you want to use, click **Choose**, and then click **OK**. Note that you can use only GIF, JPEG, or PNG files that are no larger than 1MB.

Is there any way to store data such as the person's birthday or job title?

Yes, the Contacts application offers a number of other fields, including Birthday, Job Title, Nickname, Prefix, and Suffix. To add a field to an existing contact, click the contact and then click **Edit**. Click **Add Field**, click the field you want, and then edit the field data. Note that you can also add more instances of some fields by clicking the green plus icon (🟢) to the right of a field.

Manage Your Schedule with MobileMe

You can use MobileMe to manage your schedule. Using the Calendar application, you can add events (appointments and all-day activities) and to-do items (tasks).

If you already have events in your Mac iCal application, you can synchronize them with MobileMe. See "Synchronize Your Mac with MobileMe," later in this chapter.

Manage Your Schedule with MobileMe

Display MobileMe Calendar

1️⃣ Log in to your MobileMe account.

Note: *See the "Log in to MobileMe" section, earlier in this chapter.*

2️⃣ Click **Switch Apps** (▭).

3️⃣ Click **Calendar** (📅).

Navigate Calendar

1️⃣ Click **Next Month** (▶) until the month you want appears.

● Click **Previous Month** (◀) to move back to the month you want.

2️⃣ Click the date.

● To see just that date, click **Day**.

● To see the date in the context of its week, click **Week**.

● To see the date in the context of its month, click **Month**.

● To return to today's date, click **Today**.

Create an Event

1. Navigate to the date when the event occurs.

2. Click the calendar you want to use.

3. Double-click the time when the event starts.

● Calendar adds a one-hour event.

Note: *If the event is less than or more than an hour, you can also click and drag the mouse ( ) over the full appointment period.*

4. Type the name of the event.

5. Press Return.

Edit an Event

1. Double-click the event.

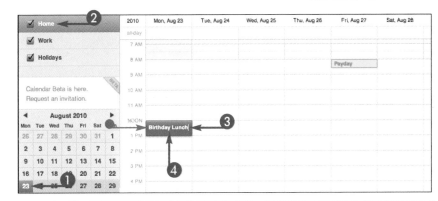

2. Edit the event details as needed.

● If the event lasts all day, click **All-Day Event** (changes to).

3. Click **OK**.

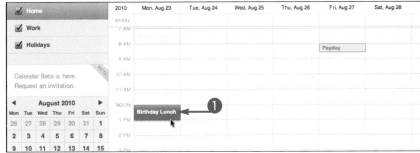
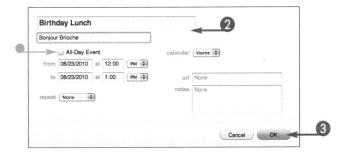

TIPS

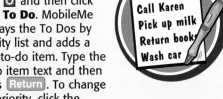

How do I create a to-do item?

Click and then click **New To Do**. MobileMe displays the To Dos by Priority list and adds a new to-do item. Type the to-do item text and then press Return. To change the priority, click the **Priority** icon ( ) on the right of the to-do item and then click **None, Low, Medium,** or **High**.

How do I change the time zone?

Click and then click **Preferences** to open the Calendar preferences. Click the **Advanced** tab and then click **Turn on time zone support** (changes to). Click the **Time zone** menu and then click the time zone you want to use. Click **Save**. MobileMe reloads and displays the new time zone in the browser's title bar.

Share Photos with MobileMe

You can use MobileMe to upload photos and share them with others. Using the Gallery application, you can create different photo albums and make those albums available for others to see.

You can also configure a photo album to allow others to upload and download photos.

Share Photos with MobileMe

Create a Photo Album

1 Log in to your MobileMe account.

Note: See the "Log in to MobileMe" section, earlier in this chapter.

2 Click **Switch Apps** (📷).

3 Click **Gallery** (🖼).

4 Click **Create a New Album** (⊞).

5 Type the album name.

6 To allow downloading, click **Downloading of photos or entire album** (☐ changes to ☑).

7 To allow Web uploading, click **Uploading of photos via web browser** (☐ changes to ☑).

8 To allow e-mail uploading, click **Adding of photos via email or iPhone** (☐ changes to ☑).

9 Click **Create**.

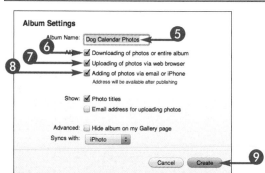

Upload Photos

1 Click the album.

2 Click **Upload** ().

The Uploads window appears.

3 Click **Close window when complete** (☐ changes to ☑).

4 Click **Choose**.

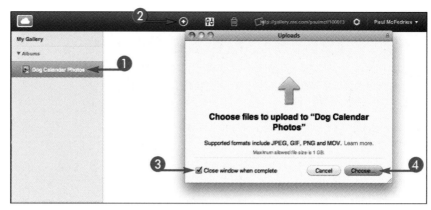

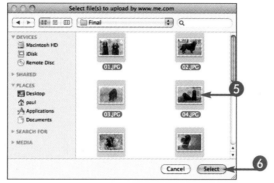

5 Select the photos you want to upload.

Note: *To select multiple photos, press and hold* ⌘ *and click each photo. To select all the folders in the current folder, press* ⌘ + A.

6 Click **Select**.

MobileMe uploads the photos to the album.

Can I upload photos to an album using my iPhone?

Yes, as long as you are using the iPhone 2.0 or later software. On your iPhone's Home screen, tap **Photos**, tap the photo album that contains the photo you want to upload, tap the photo, tap the **Action** icon in the lower left corner, and then tap **Send to MobileMe**. Tap the album you want to use for the photo. In the new e-mail message, type a photo title in the Subject field and then tap **Send**.

How do people view my MobileMe Gallery?

People can view your MobileMe Gallery using any Web browser. The address of your gallery is shown in the upper right corner of the Gallery application. The format is http://gallery. me.com/*username*, where *username* is your MobileMe username.

Upload Files to Your iDisk

You can store files with your MobileMe account by using the iDisk online storage feature. With iDisk, you upload files from your Mac and store them in iDisk folders such as Pictures, Documents, and Backup.

You can use iDisk to make backup copies of important documents. Because you can access your iDisk from any computer over the Web, you can also use iDisk to make certain files available to you from any location that has Internet access.

Upload Files to Your iDisk

Display MobileMe iDisk

1 Log in to your MobileMe account.

Note: See the "Log in to MobileMe" section, earlier in this chapter.

2 Click **Switch Apps** (▣).

3 Click **iDisk** (☁).

Upload a File Using MobileMe

1 Click the folder you want to use to store the file.

2 Click **Upload** (◉).

The Uploads window appears.

3 Click **Close window when complete** (☐ changes to ☑).

4 Click **Choose**.

⑤ Select the file you want to upload.

⑥ Click **Select**.

MobileMe uploads the file to your iDisk.

Upload a File Using Your Mac

① Log in to your MobileMe account using your Mac.

Note: See the tip in the "Log in to MobileMe" section, earlier in this chapter.

② Click **Finder** (🖥).

③ Click **iDisk**.

④ Open the folder to which you want to upload the file.

⑤ Press ⌘+N.

A new Finder window appears.

⑥ Open the folder that contains the file you want to upload.

⑦ Click and drag the file and drop it inside the iDisk folder.

Your Mac uploads the file to your iDisk.

You can now access your uploaded files online.

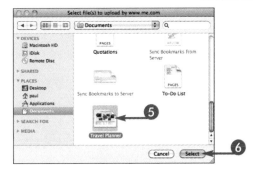

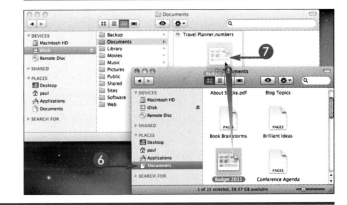

TIPS

Can I access my iDisk from Windows?

Yes, if you also have a Windows computer at home or at work, you can use it to access your iDisk. Open a Web browser and enter the address **http://idisk.me.com/*username*/**, where *username* is your MobileMe member name. When Windows asks you to log on, type your MobileMe member name and password, and then click **Log In**.

Can I use iDisk to share files with other people over the Web?

Yes. Click the file you want to share and then click **Share File**. In the Sharing dialog that appears, type the contact names or e-mail addresses of the people you want to share the file with, type a short message, and then click **Share**. You can use the Public folder to do this. Other people can then use a Web browser to enter the address http://public.me.com/*username*/, where *username* is your MobileMe member name.

Synchronize Your Mac with MobileMe

You can ensure that your Mac and your MobileMe account have the same data by synchronizing the two. You can synchronize bookmarks, iCal appointments, Address Book contacts, e-mail accounts, and more.

If you have a second Mac, you can also synchronize it with the same MobileMe account, which ensures that your two Macs use the same data.

Synchronize Your Mac with MobileMe

① Click the **Apple** icon ().

② Click **System Preferences**.

Note: *You can also open System Preferences by clicking its icon () on the Dock.*

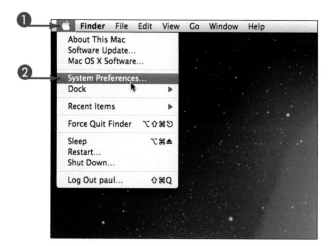

The System Preferences window appears.

③ Click **MobileMe**.

Note: *If you see Are You a MobileMe Member?, type your MobileMe member name and password and then click **Sign In**.*

The MobileMe preferences appear.

④ Click **Sync**.

⑤ Click **Synchronize with MobileMe** (changes to ☑).

● Your Mac registers itself with your MobileMe account.

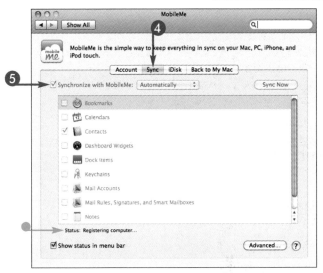

⑥ Click the check box beside each type of data you want to synchronize (changes to ☑).

⑦ Click **Sync Now**.

Your Mac synchronizes the data with your MobileMe account.

TIPS

Is there a way to have my Mac synchronize with my MobileMe account on a schedule?

Yes, you can configure your MobileMe preferences to perform an automatic synchronization at regular intervals. Follow Steps 1 to 6 to enable the synchronization. In the Synchronize with MobileMe pop-up menu, click and then click the interval you want: **Every Hour**, **Every Day**, or **Every Week**.

What happens if I modify an appointment, contact, bookmark, or other data in MobileMe?

The synchronization process works both ways. That is, all the Mac data you selected to synchronize is sent to your MobileMe account. However, the data on your MobileMe account is also sent to your Mac. This means that if you modify, add, or delete data on your MobileMe account, those changes are also reflected in your Mac data.

Customizing Your Mac

Mac OS X comes with a number of features that enable you to customize your Mac. Not only can you change the appearance of your Mac to suit your taste, but you can also change the way your Mac works to make it easier and more efficient for you to use.

Display System Preferences

You can find many of the Mac OS X customization features in the System Preferences, a collection of settings and options that control the overall look and operation of Mac OS X. To use these settings, you must know how to display the System Preferences window.

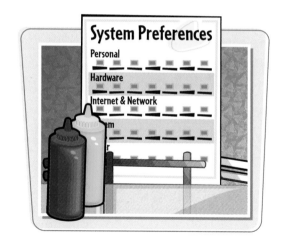

Display System Preferences

Open System Preferences

1 Click the **Apple** icon (⬛).

2 Click **System Preferences**.

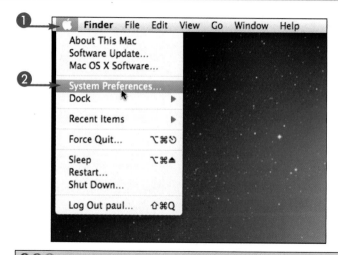

The System Preferences window appears.

Close System Preferences

① Click **System Preferences**.

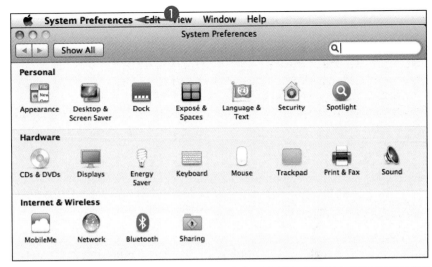

② Click **Quit System Preferences**.

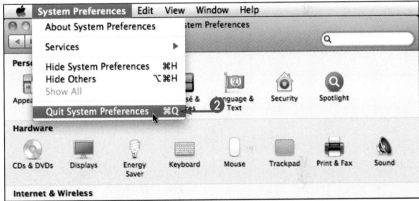

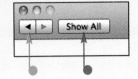

Are there faster methods I can use to open and close System Preferences?
The fastest way to start System Preferences is to click the **System Preferences** icon (🖥) in the Dock. Probably the fastest method you can use to quit System Preferences is to click 🖥. Alternatively, Control +click or right-click 🖥 and then click **Quit**. Finally, if your hands are closer to the keyboard than to the mouse, you can quit System Preferences by pressing ⌘+Q.

Sometimes when I open System Preferences I do not see all the icons. How can I restore the original icons?
When you click an icon in System Preferences, the window changes to show just the options and settings associated with that icon. To return to the main System Preferences window, press ⌘+L or use either of the following techniques:

● Click ◀ until the main window appears.

● Click **Show All**.

Change the Desktop Background

To give your Mac a different look, you can change the desktop background to display either a different image or a solid color.

You can change the desktop background to show either a fixed image or a series of images that change periodically.

Set a Fixed Background Image

1 Open System Preferences.

Note: See the "Display System Preferences" section, earlier in this chapter.

2 Click **Desktop & Screen Saver**.

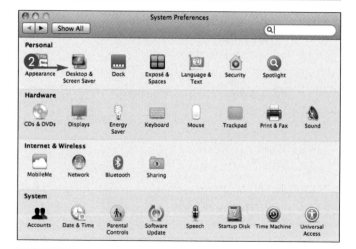

The Desktop & Screen Saver preferences appear.

3 Click **Desktop**.

4 Click the image category you want to use.

5 Click the image you want to use as the desktop background.

Your Mac changes the desktop background.

6 If you chose a photo in Step **5**, click 🔼 and then click an item to determine how your Mac displays the photo.

Note: Another way to set a fixed background image is to select a photo in iPhoto, click **Share***, and then click* **Set Desktop***.*

Set a Changing Background Image

1 Click **Change picture** (☐ changes to ☑).

2 Click 🔼 in the pop-up menu and then click how often you want the background image to change.

3 If you want your Mac to choose the periodic image randomly, click **Random order** (☐ changes to ☑).

Your Mac changes the desktop background periodically based on your chosen interval.

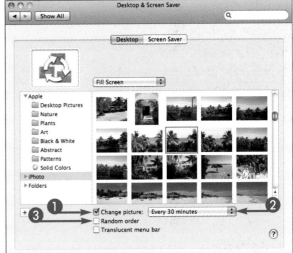

 TIP

When I choose a photo, what is the difference between the various options for displaying the photo?

Your Mac gives you five options for displaying the photo:

- **Fill Screen**: This option expands the photo by the same amount in all four directions until it fills the entire desktop. This option can cause some edges of the photo to be cropped out.

- **Fit to Screen**: This option expands the photo in all four directions until the photo is either the same height as the desktop or the same width as the desktop.

- **Stretch to Fill Screen**: This option expands the photo in all four directions until it fills the entire desktop. Because the photo is usually expanded more either vertically or horizontally, this option can cause the photo to appear distorted.

- **Center**: This option displays the photo at its actual size and places the photo in the center of the desktop.

- **Tile**: This option repeats your photo multiple times to fill the entire desktop.

Activate the Screen Saver

You can set up Mac OS X to display a *screen saver*, a moving pattern or series of pictures. The screen saver appears after your computer has been idle for a while.

If you leave your monitor on for long stretches while your computer is idle, a faint version of the unmoving image can endure for a while on the screen, a phenomenon known as *persistence*. A screen saver prevents this by displaying a moving image.

Activate the Screen Saver

① Open System Preferences.

Note: See the "Display System Preferences" section, earlier in this chapter.

② Click **Desktop & Screen Saver**.

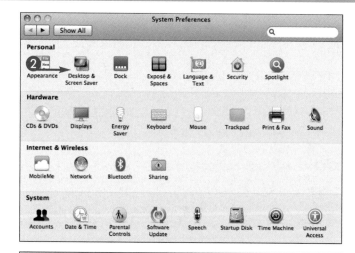

The Desktop & Screen Saver preferences appear.

③ Click **Screen Saver**.

④ Click the screen saver you want to use.

● A preview of the screen saver appears here.

⑤ Click and drag the **Start screen saver** slider (▢) to set when the screen saver begins.

Note: The interval you choose is the number of minutes or hours that your Mac must be idle before the screen saver starts.

● If the screen saver is customizable, click **Options** to configure it.

● If you also want to see the current time when the screen saver is active, click **Show with clock** (☐ changes to ☑).

● If you want to see a different screen saver each time, click **Use random screen saver** (☐ changes to ☑).

TIP

What are hot corners and how do I configure them?

A *hot corner* is a corner of your Mac's screen that you have set up to perform some action when you move the mouse (🖰) to that corner. To configure hot corners, follow these steps:

1 Follow Steps **1** to **4** to select a screen saver.

2 Click **Hot Corners**.

System Preferences displays the Active Screen Corners dialog.

3 In the top left pop-up menu, click 🔽 and then click the action you want to perform when you move 🖰 to the top left corner of the screen.

4 Click 🔽 and then click the action you want to perform when you move 🖰 to the top right corner of the screen.

5 Click 🔽 and then click the action you want to perform when you move 🖰 to the bottom left corner of the screen.

6 Click 🔽 and then click the action you want to perform when you move 🖰 to the bottom right corner of the screen.

7 Click **OK**.

Set Your Mac's Sleep Options

You can make Mac OS X more energy efficient by putting the display or your entire Mac to sleep after a period of inactivity.

Sleep mode means that your display or your Mac is in a temporary low-power mode. This saves energy on all Macs, and also saves battery power on a notebook Mac.

Set Your Mac's Sleep Options

Open the Energy Saver Preferences

1 Open System Preferences.

Note: See the "Display System Preferences" section, earlier in this chapter.

2 Click **Energy Saver**.

The Energy Saver preferences appear.

Set Sleep Options for a Desktop Mac

1 Click and drag 🔘 to set the Computer sleep timer.

This specifies the period of inactivity after which your computer goes to sleep.

2 Click and drag 🔘 to set the Display sleep timer.

This specifies the period of inactivity after which your display goes to sleep.

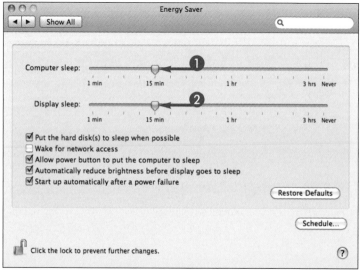

Set Sleep Options for a Notebook Mac

1 Click **Battery**.

2 Click and drag ▽ to set the Computer sleep timer for when your Mac is on battery power.

3 Click and drag ▽ to set the Display sleep timer for when your Mac is on battery power.

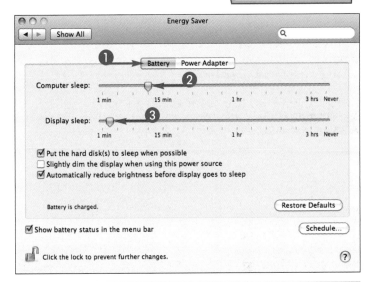

4 Click **Power Adapter**.

5 Click and drag ▽ to set the Computer sleep timer for when your Mac is plugged in.

6 Click and drag ▽ to set the Display sleep timer for when your Mac is plugged in.

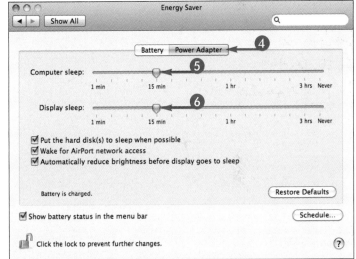

TIPS

How do I wake up a sleeping display or computer?

If your Mac's display is in sleep mode, you can wake up the display either by moving your mouse or by pressing a key such as ⌘, Control, or Shift on your keyboard. If your entire Mac is in sleep mode, you wake up the computer either by clicking the mouse or by pressing a key such as ⌘, Control, or Shift on your keyboard.

I changed the Display sleep timer, and now I never see my screen saver. Why?

You have set the Display sleep timer to a time that is less than your screen saver timer. For example, suppose you have configured Mac OS X to switch on the screen saver after 15 minutes. If you then set the Display sleep timer to a shorter interval, such as 10 minutes, Mac OS X will always put the display to sleep before the screen saver has a chance to kick in. Set the Display sleep timer longer than your screen saver timer.

Change the Display Resolution

You can change the resolution of the Mac OS X display. This enables you to adjust the display for best viewing or for maximum compatibility with whatever application you are using.

You can change the Mac OS X display resolution using either the System Preferences window or the menu bar.

Change Resolution via the Display Preferences

① Open System Preferences.

Note: See the "Display System Preferences" section, earlier in this chapter.

② Click **Displays**.

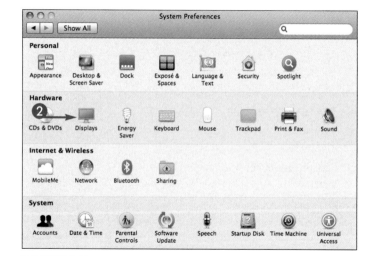

The Color LCD preferences appear.

③ Click **Display**.

④ Click the resolution you want to use.

Your Mac adjusts the screen to the new resolution.

● To change the resolution using your Mac's menu bar, as described on the next page, click **Show displays in menu bar** (□ changes to ☑).

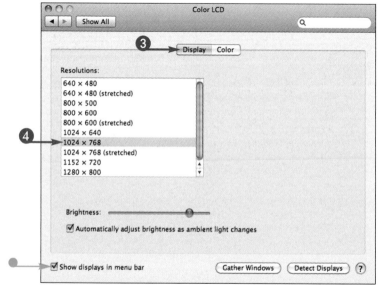

Change Resolution via the Menu Bar

1 Click the **Displays** icon (■).

Your Mac opens a menu that shows the most commonly or recently used resolutions.

● The resolution with the check mark (☑) is the current resolution.

2 Click the resolution you want to use.

Your Mac adjusts the screen to the new resolution.

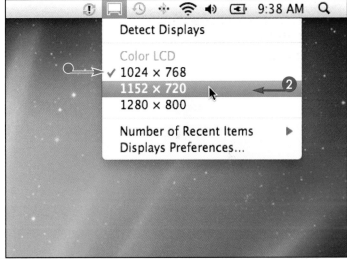

What do the resolution numbers mean?

The resolution numbers are expressed in *pixels*, short for picture elements, which are the individual dots that make up what you see on your Mac's screen. The pixels are arranged in rows and columns, and the resolution tells you the number of pixels in each row and column. So a resolution of 1024 × 768 means that the display is using 1,024-pixel rows and 768-pixel columns.

Why do some resolutions also include the word "stretched"?

Most older displays are made with the ratio of the width to the height — this is called the *aspect ratio* — set at 4:3. However, most new Mac displays are made with an aspect ratio of 16:10, which is called *widescreen*. Resolutions designed for 4:3 displays — such as 800 × 600 and 1024 × 768 — take up only part of a widescreen display. To make them take up the entire display, choose the *stretched* version of the resolution.

Change Your Mac's Name

You can give your Mac a distinctive or easier name. By default, your Mac's computer name is your name followed by *'s Mac* — for example, Karen Hammond's Mac.

You can also change your Mac's network name, which is the computer name with spaces replaced with hyphens (-), other symbols removed, and *.local* added — for example, Karen-Hammonds-Mac.local. Both tasks require an administrator account.

Change Your Mac's Name

Change Your Mac's Computer Name

1 Open System Preferences.

Note: *See the "Display System Preferences" section, earlier in this chapter.*

2 Click **Sharing**.

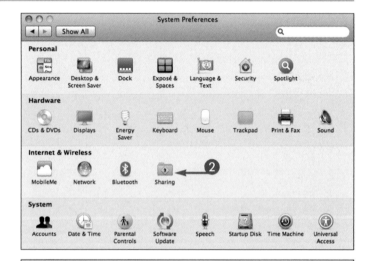

The Sharing preferences appear.

3 Use the Computer Name text box to type the name you want to use.

4 Press Return.

Your Mac sets the new computer name.

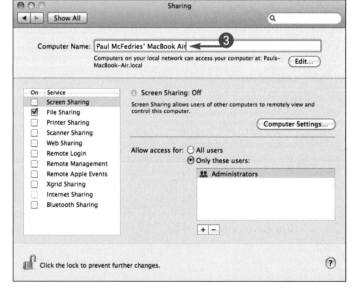

Change Your Mac's Network Name

5 Click **Edit**.

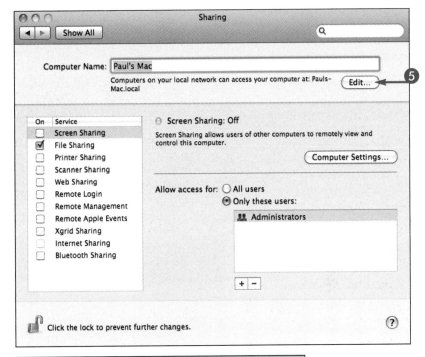

6 Use the Local Hostname text box to type the network name you want to use.

Note: *You cannot edit the .local part of the network name.*

7 Click **OK**.

Your Mac sets the new network name.

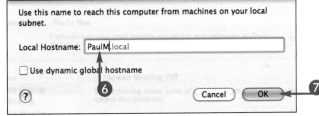

 TIPS

Are there any restrictions on the computer name or network name?

Yes. The computer name must be 63 characters or less and can include any character except at (@), equals (=), and colon (:). The network name must be 63 characters or less and it can use only letters, numbers, and hyphens (-).

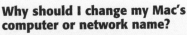

Why should I change my Mac's computer or network name?

If you activate file sharing as described in Chapter 13, your Mac's computer name appears in Finder's sidebar and in the Network folder. A different name might make it easier for other people to access or find your Mac on your network. Other people can use the network name to connect to your Mac manually, so a shorter name makes this easier.

Customize the Dock

You can make the Dock take up less room on the screen, or you can make the Dock easier to access and use, by modifying a few Dock preferences.

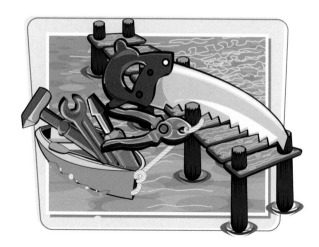

1 Open System Preferences.

Note: See the "Display System Preferences" section, earlier in this chapter.

2 Click **Dock**.

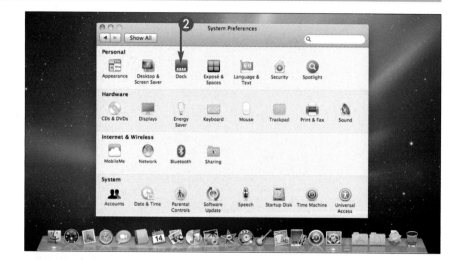

The Dock preferences appear.

3 Click and drag the **Size** 🔘 to make the Dock smaller or larger.

● You can also click and drag the Dock divider: Drag up to increase the Dock size; drag down to decrease the Dock size.

● System Preferences adjusts the size of the Dock.

Note: If your Dock is already as wide as the screen, dragging the Size slider to the right (toward the Large value) has no effect.

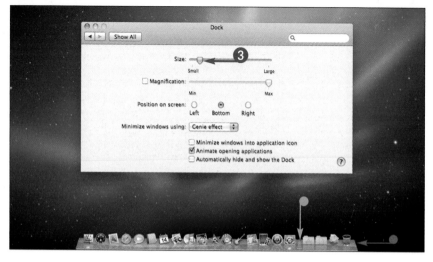

④ Click **Magnification** (☐ changes to ☑).

⑤ Click and drag the **Magnification** slider (◉) to set the magnification level.

● When you position the mouse (↖) over a Dock icon, your Mac magnifies the icon.

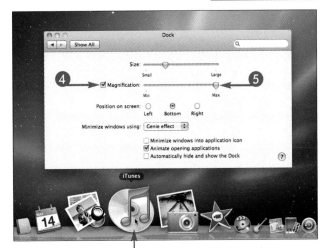

⑥ Use the **Position on screen** options to click where you want the Dock to appear, such as the **Left** side of the screen (○ changes to ◉).

● Your Mac moves the Dock to the new position.

⑦ In the **Minimize windows using** pop-up menu, click ◉ and then click the effect you want your Mac to use when you minimize a window: **Genie effect** or **Scale effect**.

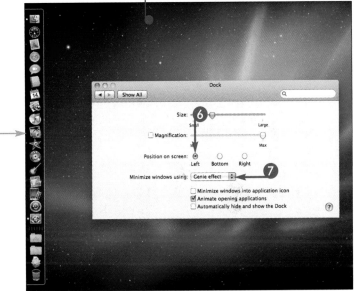

TIP

Are there easier methods I can use to control some of these preferences?

Yes, your Mac gives you an easier way to turn Dock magnification on and off and to change the Dock position. Click the **Apple** icon (🍎) and then click **Dock**. Click **Turn Magnification On** to enable the magnification feature; click **Turn Magnification Off** to disable this feature. You can also click the **Position on Left** command, the **Position on Bottom** command, or the **Position on Right** command to change the Dock position. You can also click **Dock Preferences** to open System Preferences' Dock window.

Add an Icon to the Dock

You can enhance the convenience of the Dock by adding an icon for an application you use frequently. The icon remains in the Dock even when the application is closed, so you can always open the application with a single click.

You can add an icon to the Dock even if the program is not currently running.

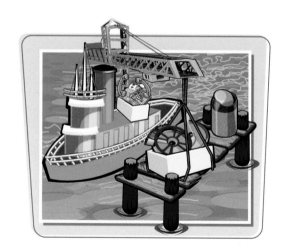

Add an Icon to the Dock

Add an Icon for a Nonrunning Application

① Click **Finder** (🖥).

② Click **Applications**.

③ Click and drag the application icon, and then drop it inside the Dock.

● Be sure to drop the icon to the left of the Dock divider.

● Mac OS X adds the application's icon to the Dock.

Add an Icon for a Running Application

1 Control +click or right-click the application icon in the Dock.

2 Click **Options**.

3 Click **Keep in Dock**.

The application's icon remains in the Dock even after you close the program.

Is there a way to get my Mac to start the application automatically each time I log in to the computer?

Login Items
✓ **Lotus Notes**
✓ **Illustrator**
✓ **iView**
✓ **Photoshop**

Yes, your Mac maintains a list of *login items*, which are applications that run automatically after you log in. You can configure your application as a login item, and your Mac opens it automatically each time you log in. Control +click or right-click the application's Dock icon, click **Options**, and then click **Open at Login**.

How do I remove an icon from the Dock?

Control +click or right-click the application's Dock icon, click **Options**, and then click **Remove from Dock**. If the application is currently running, Mac OS X removes the icon from the Dock when you quit the program. Note that you can remove any Dock icon except Finder (⊞) and Trash (🗑). Removing an application's Dock icon does not delete the application itself.

Hide
the Dock

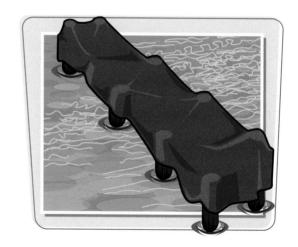

If you would like more room on the Mac OS X screen to display your applications, you can hide the Dock to free up some screen space.

When the Dock is hidden, it is still easily accessible whenever you need to use it.

Hide the Dock

Turn On Dock Hiding

① Click [].

② Click **Dock**.

③ Click **Turn Hiding On**.

● You can also (Control)+click or right-click the Dock divider and then click **Turn Hiding On**.

● Mac OS X removes the Dock from the desktop.

Display the Dock Temporarily

1 Move the mouse (k) to the bottom of the screen.

● Mac OS X temporarily displays the Dock.

Note: *To hide the Dock again, move the mouse (k) away from the bottom of the screen.*

TIPS

How do I stop hiding the Dock?

When you no longer need the extra screen space for your applications, you can turn off Dock hiding to bring the Dock back into view. Click 📷, click **Dock**, and then click **Turn Hiding Off**.

Is there a faster way to hide the Dock?

Yes. You can quickly hide the Dock by pressing Option + ⌘ + D. This keyboard shortcut is a toggle, which means that you can also turn off Dock hiding by pressing Option + ⌘ + D. When the Dock is hidden, you can display it temporarily by pressing Control + F3 (on some keyboards you must press Fn + Control + F3).

Add a Widget to the Dashboard

You can make the Dashboard better by customizing it to include any widgets that you find useful or informative.

A *widget* is a mini-application, particularly one designed to perform a single task, such as displaying the weather, showing stock data, or providing sports scores.

Add a Widget to the Dashboard

① Click **Finder** (▨).

② Click **Applications**.

③ Double-click **Dashboard**.

Your Mac displays the Dashboard and its current set of widgets.

④ Click **Add** (⊕).

Your Mac displays its collection of widgets.

⑤ Use the arrows (◄ and ►) to scroll to the widget you want to add.

⑥ Click the widget.

● Your Mac adds the widget to the Dashboard.

⑦ Use the mouse (▶) to click and drag the widget to the position you prefer.

● If the widget is configurable, it displays an *i* when you position the mouse (▶) over the widget.

⑧ Click the *i*.

⑨ Configure the widget as needed.

⑩ Click **Done**.

⑪ Click the desktop.

Your Mac closes the Dashboard.

TIPS

Are there faster methods I can use to open the Dashboard?

The fastest way to start the Dashboard is to click the **Dashboard** icon (⊙) in the Dock. If your hands are on the keyboard, you can also display the Dashboard quickly on most Macs by pressing F4. On some keyboards, you must press Fn + F4 instead. Note that you can also press F4 (or Fn + F4) to close the Dashboard.

How do I remove a widget from the Dashboard?

Dashboard gives you a couple of ways to remove widgets. If you just want to remove a single widget, press and hold Option, position the mouse (▶) over the widget, and then click the **Close** button (☒) that Dashboard displays in the upper left corner of the widget. If you want to remove more than one widget, click ⊕ to display the available widgets, and then click ☒ in each widget that you want to remove.

Networking with Your Mac

If you have multiple computers in your home or office, you can set up these computers as a network to share information and equipment. Assuming you already have your computers connected, this chapter shows you how to work with the other computers on your network, and how to share your Mac's resources with other network users.

Understanding Networking

A *network* is a collection of computers that are connected using either a cable hookup or a wireless hookup. A network gives you a number of advantages, such as being able to share files and equipment.

Share Files

Networked computers are connected to each other, and so they can exchange files with each other along the connection. This enables people to share information and to collaborate on projects. Mac OS X includes built-in security, so that you can control what files you share with other people.

Share Equipment

Computers connected over a network can share some types of equipment. For example, one computer can share its printer, which enables other network users to send their documents to that printer. Networked computers can also share hard drives, CD or DVD drives, and document scanners.

Wired Networking

Network Cable

A *network cable* is a special cable designed for exchanging information. One end of the cable plugs into the Mac's network port. The other end plugs into a network connection point, which is usually the network's router (discussed next), but it could also be a switch, hub, or even another Mac. Information, shared files, and other network data travel through the network cables.

Router

A *router* is a central connection point for all of the computers on the wired portion of the network. For each computer, you run a network cable from the Mac's network port to a port in the router.

When network data travels from computer A to computer B, it first goes out through computer A's network port, along its network cable, and into the router. Then the router passes the data along computer B's network cable and into its network port.

Wireless Networking

Wireless Connections

A *wireless network* is a collection of two or more computers that communicate with each other using radio signals instead of cable. The most common wireless technology is Wi-Fi (rhymes with hi-fi) or 802.11. There are three main types — 802.11b, 802.11g, and 802.11n — each of which has its own range and speed limits. The other common wireless technology is Bluetooth, which enables devices to communicate directly with each other.

Wireless Access Point

A *wireless access point* (WAP) is a device that receives and transmits signals from wireless computers to form a wireless network. Many WAPs also accept wired connections, which enables both wired and wireless computers to form a network. If your network has a broadband modem, you can connect the modem to a type of WAP called a *wireless gateway,* which extends Internet access to all of the computers on the network.

273

Connect to a Wireless Network

If your Mac has built-in wireless networking capabilities, you can use them to connect to a wireless network that is within range. This could be a network in your home, your office, or a public location such as a coffee shop.

Most wireless networks have security turned on, which means you must know the correct password to connect to the network.

Connect to a Wireless Network

① Click the **AirPort status** icon (📶) in the menu bar.

Note: AirPort is the name that Apple uses for its line of wireless networking devices.

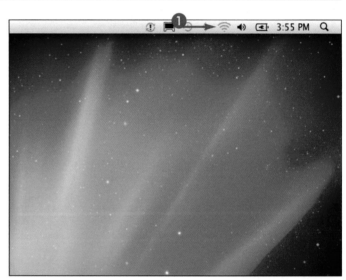

Your Mac locates the wireless networks within range of your Mac.

● The available networks appear in the menu.

● Networks with a Lock icon (🔒) require a password to join.

② Click the wireless network you want to join.

If the wireless network is secure, your Mac prompts you for the password.

③ Use the Password text box to type the network password.

● If the password is very long, you can click **Show password** (□ changes to ☑) to see the actual characters instead of dots. This helps to ensure you type the password correctly.

④ Click **OK**.

Your Mac connects to the wireless network.

● The AirPort status icon changes from ⌢ to ⌢ to indicate the connection.

TIPS

I know a particular network is within range, but I do not see it in the list. Why not?

As a security precaution, some wireless networks do not broadcast their availability. However, you can still connect to such a network, assuming you know its name and the password, if one is required. Click ⌢ and then click **Join Other Network**. Use the Network Name text box to type the name of the network, click the **Security** ⬍, and then click the network's security type. Follow Steps **3** and **4** to join the network.

I do not see the AirPort status icon on my menu bar. How do I display the icon?

You can do this using System Preferences. Click its icon (⬜) in the Dock (or click ⬜ and then click **System Preferences**) to open the System Preferences window. Click **Network**, click **AirPort**, and then click the **Show AirPort status in menu bar** check box (□ changes to ☑).

Connect to a Network Resource

To see what other network users have shared on the network, you can use the Network folder to view the other computers and then connect to them to see their shared resources.

To get full access to a Mac's shared resources, you must connect with a username and password for an administrator account on that Mac. Note, too, that your Mac can also connect to Windows computers.

Connect to a Network Resource

① Click **Finder** (🖥).

② Click **Go**.

③ Click **Network**.

Note: *Another way to run the Network command is to press* Shift + ⌘ + K .

The Network folder appears.

● Each icon represents a computer on your local network.

④ Double-click the computer you want to connect to.

Your Mac connects to the network computer using the Guest account.

Note: *The Guest account has only limited access to the network computer and only limited privileges to work with shared resources on that computer.*

⑤ Click **Connect As**.

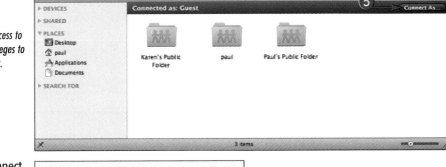

Your Mac prompts you to connect to the network computer as a registered user.

⑥ Use the Name text box to type the user name of an account on the network computer.

⑦ Use the Password text box to type the password of the account.

⑧ To store the account data, click **Remember this password in my keychain** (□ changes to ☑).

⑨ Click **Connect**.

Your Mac connects to the computer and shows the shared resources that you can access.

⑩ When you are done, click **Disconnect**.

TIPS

Is there a faster way to connect to a network computer?

Yes. If your Mac detects network computers sharing resources, it usually displays the names of those computers in Finder's sidebar area, under the Shared section. Click the computer you want to connect with (●) and then follow Steps **5** through **9** to connect as a registered user.

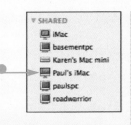

How can I connect to a computer that does not appear in the Network folder?

If you are sure that the computer is sharing resources on the network, `Control`+click or right-click **Finder** (🖼), and then click **Connect to Server**. In the Connect to Server dialog, use the Server Address text box to type the address: for a Mac, type the Mac's network name followed by **.local**; for a Windows PC, type **smb://** followed by the PC's name; for any computer, type its IP address. Click **Connect**.

Turn On File and Printer Sharing

You can share your files and printers with other network users. This enables those users to access your files and print on your printers over the network. Before you can share these resources, you must turn on your Mac's file- and printer-sharing features.

To learn how to share a particular folder, see "Share a Folder" later in this chapter; to learn how to share a particular printer, see "Share a Printer" later in this chapter.

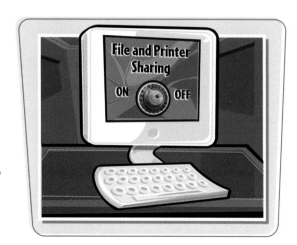

Turn On File and Printer Sharing

① Click the **Apple** icon ().

② Click **System Preferences**.

Note: You can also click System Preferences ( ) in the Dock.

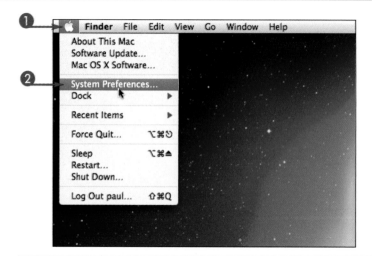

The System Preferences window appears.

③ Click **Sharing**.

The Sharing preferences appear.

4 Click the **File Sharing** check box
(☐ changes to ☑).

Note: *If your Mac is set up to go into sleep mode after an idle period, a message appears to remind you of this. Click **OK**.*

You can now share your folders, as described in the next section.

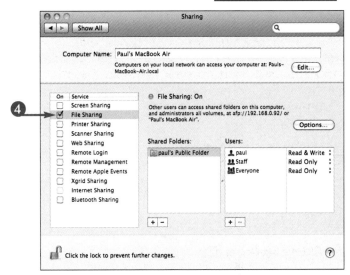

5 Click the **Printer Sharing** check box (☐ changes to ☑).

You can now share your printers, as described later in this chapter.

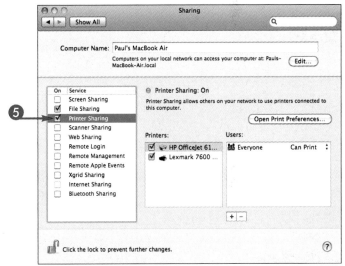

TIPS

Another user has asked me for my Mac's IP address. How do I look that up?

192.168.0.54

Your Mac gives you a couple of ways to do this. Follow Steps 1 to 3 in this section, click **File Sharing** (click the name, not the check box); the series of digits after afp:// is your IP address (such as 192.168.0.92). Alternatively, follow Steps 1 and 2, click **Network**, click **Ethernet** (or click **AirPort** if you have a wireless network connection), and then read the IP Address value.

What is the Public folder and how do I access it?

Public Folder

Your user account's Public folder is a special folder that you use to share files with other people on the network or on your Mac. If someone connects to your Mac using your user name and password, he or she has full access to the Public folder. Everyone else can only read the contents of the folder or add files to the Drop Box folder. To access the folder, click **Finder** (🖥️), click your username, and then open the Public folder.

279

Share a Folder

You can share one of your folders on the network, enabling other network users to view and optionally edit the files you place in that folder.

Mac OS X automatically shares your Public folder, but you can share other folders. Sharing a folder enables you to work on a file with other people without having to send them a copy of the file.

Share a Folder

① Click ![apple icon].

② Click **System Preferences**.

Note: You can also click System Preferences (![icon]) in the Dock.

The System Preferences window appears.

③ Click **Sharing**.

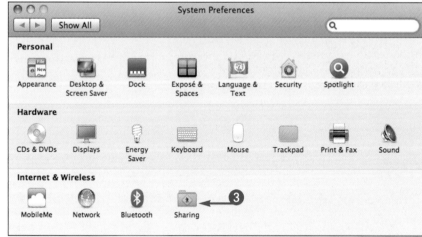

④ Click **File Sharing**.

*Note: Be sure to click the **File Sharing** text, not the check box. This ensures that you do not accidentally uncheck the check box.*

⑤ Under Shared Folders, click ⊞.

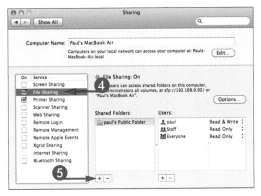

An Open dialog appears.

⑥ Click the folder you want to share.

⑦ Click **Add**.

Your Mac begins sharing the folder.

Note: You can also click and drag a folder from a Finder window and drop it on the list of shared folders.

● The folder appears in the Shared Folders list.

⑧ Click the folder.

● The current permission is indicated with a check mark (☑).

⑨ For the Everyone user, click the current permission and then click the permission you want to assign.

Mac OS X assigns the permission to the user.

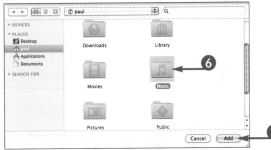

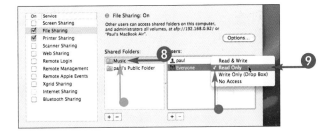

TIPS

What are the differences between the various types of permissions I can assign to users?

Permissions define what users can and cannot do with the shared folder:

- **Read & Write**: Users can open files, add new files, rename or delete existing files, and edit file contents.

- **Read Only**: Users can open files, but cannot add, delete, rename, or edit files.

- **Write Only (Drop Box)**: Users can add files to the folder as a Drop Box, but cannot open the folder.

- **No Access**: Users cannot open (or even see) the folder.

Can I share folders with Windows users?

Yes. In the Sharing window, click **Options** and then click the **Share files and folders using SMB** check box (☐ changes to ☑). Click your user account (☐ changes to ☑), use the Password text box to type your account password, click **OK**, and then click **Done**. Windows users must enter your username and password to see your shared folders.

If you have a printer connected to your Mac, you can share the printer with the network, enabling other network users to send their documents to your printer.

Sharing a printer saves money and time because you only have to purchase and configure one printer for all the computers on your network.

Share a Printer

① Click .

② Click **System Preferences**.

Note: You can also click System Preferences ( ) in the Dock.

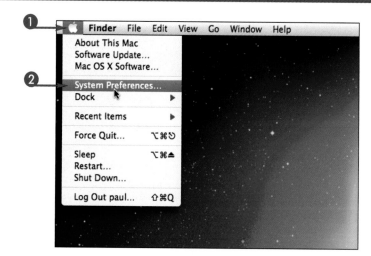

The System Preferences window appears.

③ Click **Sharing**.

④ Click **Printer Sharing**.

*Note: Be sure to click the **Printer Sharing** text, not the check box. This ensures that you do not accidentally uncheck the check box.*

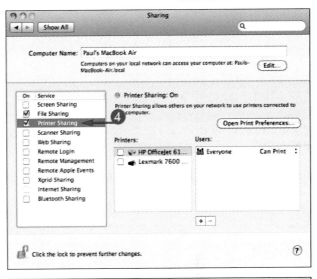

⑤ Click the check box beside the printer you want to share (☐ changes to ☑).

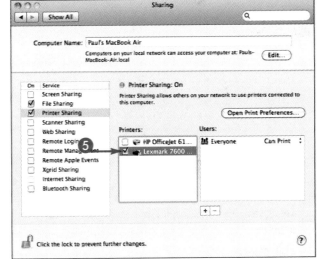

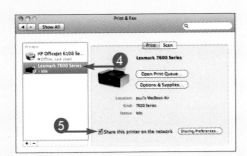

Is there another method I can use to share a printer?

Yes, you can follow these steps:

① Click .

② Click **System Preferences**.

③ Click **Print & Fax**.

④ Click the printer you want to share.

⑤ Click the **Share this printer on the network** check box (☐ changes to ☑).

Add a Shared Printer

You can send a document from your Mac to a shared printer attached to a network computer. This enables you to use just a single printer for all the computers in your network. Before you can do this, you must add a shared printer to Mac OS X.

Add a Shared Printer

① Click ▣.

② Click **System Preferences**.

Note: You can also click **System Preferences** (▣) in the Dock.

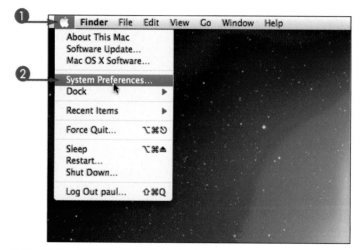

The System Preferences window appears.

③ Click **Print & Fax**.

④ Click ➕.

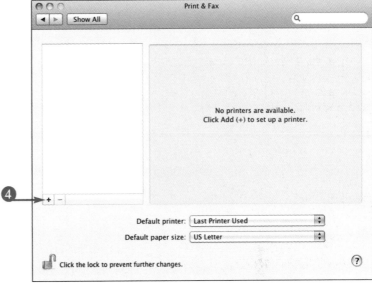

⑤ Click **Default**.

⑥ Click the shared printer.

● Look for the word *Shared* in the printer description.

⑦ Click **Add**.

Your Mac adds the printer.

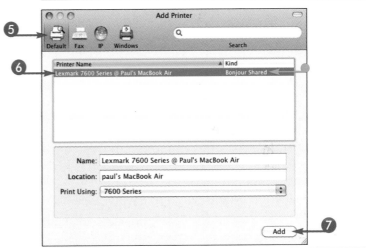

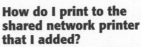

Can I add a shared Windows printer?

Yes, if you have Windows computers on your network you can connect to any printers that they share. Follow Steps **1** to **4** and then click the **Windows** tab. Click the Windows workgroup, click the computer with the shared printer, log on to the Windows computer, and then click the shared printer you want to use. In the Print Using list, click ➕, click **Select a driver to use**, and then click the printer in the list that appears. Click **Add**.

How do I print to the shared network printer that I added?

In any application that supports printing, click **File** and then click **Print**. You can also press ⌘ + P. In the Print dialog, use the Printer pop-up menu to click ➕ and then click the shared printer you added in this section. Choose any other printing options you require, and then click **Print**.

Maintaining Your Mac

To keep your Mac running smoothly, maintain top performance, and reduce the risk of computer problems, you need to perform some routine maintenance chores. This chapter shows you how to empty the trash, delete unnecessary files, update applications, back up your files, and more.

Empty the Trash

When you delete a file, your Mac sends it to the Trash folder. You can free up disk space on your Mac by periodically emptying the Trash folder.

You should empty the Trash folder at least once a month.

Empty the Trash

1. Click **Finder** (🖥).

2. Click **Finder** from the menu.

3. Click **Empty Trash**.

● You can also `Control`+click or right-click the **Trash** icon (🗑) and then click **Empty Trash**.

Note: Another way to select the Empty Trash command is to press `Shift` + `⌘` + `Del` .

Mac OS X asks you to confirm.

4. Click **Empty Trash**.

Mac OS X empties the trash (🗑 changes to 🗑).

Organize Your Desktop

If you use the Mac OS X desktop to store files and copies of documents, the desktop can become cluttered, making it hard to find the icon you want. You can make your desktop easier to navigate by organizing the icons.

Organize Your Desktop

1 Click the desktop.

2 Click **View**.

3 Click **Arrange By**.

4 Click **Name**.

You can also Control +click or right-click the desktop, click **Arrange By**, and then click **Name**, or press Option + ⌘ + 1.

● If you just want to nudge each icon into the nearest row and column, click **Clean Up Selection** instead.

● Your Mac organizes the icons alphabetically and arranges them in rows and columns from right to left.

Check Hard Disk Free Space

If you run out of room on your Mac's hard disk, you will not be able to install more applications or create more documents, and your Mac's performance will suffer. To ensure this does not happen, you can check how much free space your hard disk has left.

You should check your Mac's hard disk free space about once a month. If you frequently install programs, create large files, or download media, you should check your free space every couple of weeks.

Check Hard Disk Free Space

Check Free Space Using Finder

1 Click **Finder** (🖥).

2 Click **Macintosh HD**.

Note: You can also click any folder on your Mac's hard disk.

3 Read the "available" value, which tells you the amount of free space left on the hard disk.

Display Free Space on the Desktop

1 Display your Mac's HD (hard drive) icon on the desktop, as described in the first tip on the next page.

2 Click the desktop.

3 Click **View**.

4 Click **Show View Options**.

Note: You can also run the Show View Options command by pressing ⌘ + J.

The Desktop dialog appears.

5 Click **Show item info**
(☐ changes to ☑).

● Your Mac displays the amount of free hard disk space under the Macintosh HD icon.

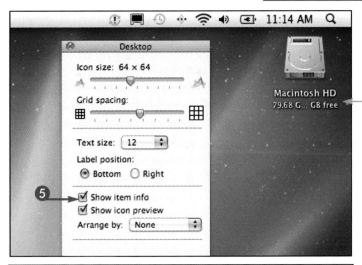

6 Drag the Icon size ◉ until you can read all the icon text.

7 Click **Close** (◉).

My Mac's hard disk icon does not appear on the desktop. How do I display it?

If you do not see the Macintosh HD icon on your desktop, click the desktop, click **Finder** in the menu bar, and then click **Preferences**. Click the **General** tab, click **Hard disks** (☐ changes to ☑), and then click **Close** (◉).

What should I do if my Mac's hard disk space is getting low?

First, you should empty the trash, as described earlier in this chapter. Next, you should uninstall any applications that you no longer use, as described in the next section. If you have any documents that you are sure you no longer need — particularly large media files — you should either move them to CD or DVD, or send them to the trash and then empty the Trash folder.

Uninstall Unused Applications

If you have an application that you no longer use, you can free up some disk space and reduce clutter in the Applications folder by uninstalling that application.

In most cases you must be logged on to Mac OS X with an administrator account to uninstall applications.

Uninstall Unused Applications

① Click **Finder** (🖥).

② Click **Applications**.

③ Click and drag the application or its folder and drop it on the **Trash** icon (■).

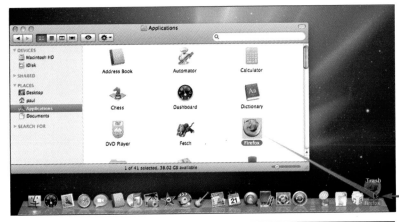

If your Mac prompts you for an administrator password, type the password, and then click **OK**.

● Your Mac uninstalls the application.

TIPS

Is there another way to uninstall an application?

Yes, in some cases. A few Mac applications come with a separate program for uninstalling the application:

① Follow Steps **1** to **3**.

② If the application has its own folder, examine the contents for an icon with "Uninstaller" in the name.

③ Double-click that icon and then follow the instructions on-screen.

Can I restore an application that I uninstalled accidentally?

If you used the application's uninstall program, the only way to restore the application is to reinstall it. If you sent the application to the trash, and that was the most recent operation you performed, click **Finder** (■), click **Edit**, and then click **Undo Move of "*Application*"** (where *Application* is the name of the application you want to restore). Otherwise, click **Trash** (■), and then use the Trash folder to click and drag the application and drop it on Applications.

Set a Software Update Schedule

Apple makes Mac OS X updates available from time to time. These updates fix problems, add new features, and resolve security issues. You can reduce computer problems and maximize online safety by setting up Mac OS X to download and install these updates automatically.

By default, Mac OS X checks for updates weekly. You can configure Software Update to check for updates daily or only once a month.

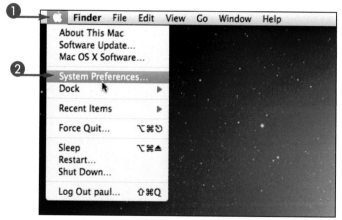

Set a Software Update Schedule

① Click ![Apple].

② Click **System Preferences**.

*Note: You can also click **System Preferences** (![icon]) in the Dock.*

The System Preferences window appears.

③ Click **Software Update**.

The Software Update preferences appear.

④ Click **Scheduled Check**.

⑤ Click **Check for updates** (☐ changes to ☑).

⑥ In the **Check for updates** pop-up menu, click ◆ and then click the schedule you want: Daily, Weekly, or Monthly.

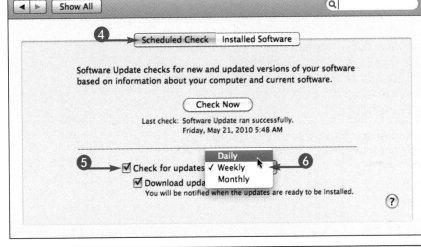

⑦ Click **Download updates automatically** (☐ changes to ☑).

Your Mac checks for updates on your selected schedule, and downloads updates automatically.

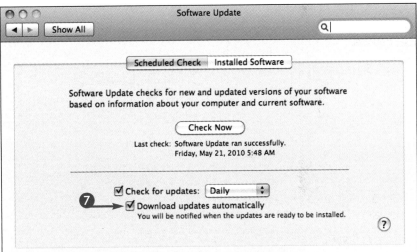

TIPS

Do I have to let my Software Update do the checking automatically?

Technically, no, you do not have to rely on Software Update's automatic checking. Instead, you can check for software updates by hand, as described in the next section. However, this is not a good idea because you should always keep your Mac software up to date, and this might not happen if you try to remember to check for updates yourself.

How does Software Update work?

When the time comes for an update check, Software Update first examines what Apple applications and system software you have installed on your Mac. Then, for each program, Software Update queries an Internet database on Apple's site to see if the program has an update available. If it does, Software Update adds the program to the update list. If the update is considered important, Software Update immediately downloads the update. The Software Update icon then bounces in the Dock to let you know that updates are available.

Update Software by Hand

Mac OS X checks for new software updates automatically on a regular schedule. If you turned off this feature or configured it to be less frequent, you can still keep Mac OS X up to date by checking for updates yourself.

See the previous section to learn how to configure the Software Update schedule.

Update Software by Hand

1 Connect to the Internet, if you have not already done so.

2 Click 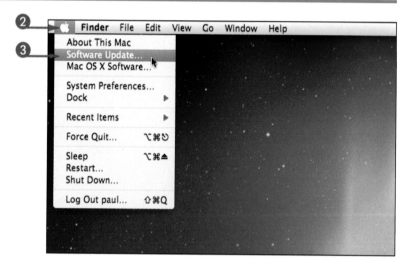.

3 Click **Software Update**.

Your Mac connects with Apple's servers and checks for new updates.

Your Mac lets you know if any software updates are available.

4 If updates are available, click **Show Details**.

Your Mac displays the list of available updates.

- A description of the selected update appears here.

- If you install any updates that display the Restart icon (■), you must restart your Mac to complete the installation.

5 Click the check box for any update you do not want to install (☑ changes to ☐).

6 Click **Install X Items** (where X is the number of updates you have selected).

For some updates, your Mac displays a software license agreement. If you see a license agreement, click **Agree**.

For some updates, your Mac asks for the administrator password.

7 Use the Password text box to type the administrator password.

8 Click **OK**.

For some updates, your Mac prompts you to restart the computer.

9 If you have any unsaved work, save and close those documents.

10 Click **Restart**.

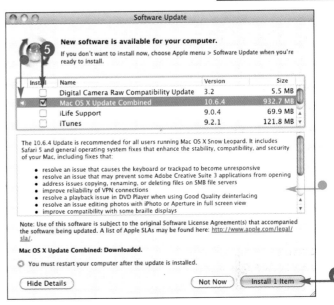

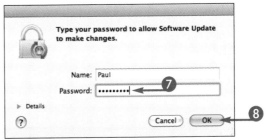

TIPS

Should I always install every available update?

As a general rule, yes, you should install every available update. However, some exceptions exist. For example, if an update is available for an application that you never use, you can safely skip that update. Also, if your Internet connection is slow, you may prefer to install the updates one at a time.

Is the Mac OS X Update important?

Yes, any update named Mac OS X Update is very important. These are major updates to your Mac's operating system, and they generally improve system stability and security. Because such an update affects your entire Mac and is usually quite large — often several hundred megabytes — it is best to install this update on its own.

Remove Unneeded Login Items

If your Mac OS X user account has login items that you no longer need, those items may slow down your Mac's startup and consume extra system memory. From time to time you should check your user account's login items and remove those you no longer need.

Only remove a login item that you are sure you do not need or that is causing a problem.

① Click ⬛.

② Click **System Preferences**.

Note: You can also click System Preferences (⬛) in the Dock.

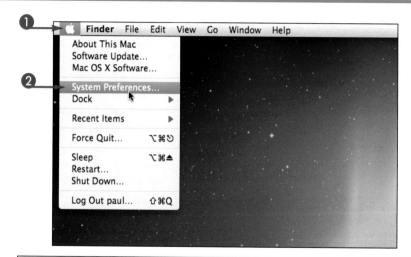

The System Preferences window appears.

③ Click **Accounts**.

④ Click your user account.

⑤ Click **Login Items**.

⑥ Click the item you want to remove.

⑦ Click ⊟.

Your Mac removes the login item.

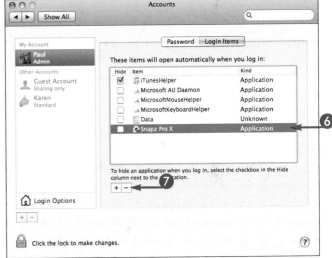

What is a login item?

When you start your Mac, many behind-the-scenes tasks get performed to set up the computer for your use. One of these tasks is that your Mac checks the list of items that are supposed to open automatically when you log in to your user account. These items are usually applications, but they can also be files, folders, and shared network locations. These are called *login items*.

Can you give me an example of a problem related to a login item?

Yes. If you uninstall an application by moving it to the trash as described earlier, the application may leave behind one or more login items, and these will cause an error each time you log in. Similarly, if a login item refers to a network resource that no longer exists, you will see an error similar to the one shown here.

Configure Time Machine Backups

Macs are reliable machines, but they do crash and all hard disks eventually die, so at some point your data will be at risk. To avoid losing that data forever, you need to configure the Mac OS X Time Machine feature to perform regular backups.

To use Time Machine, your Mac requires a second hard disk. This can be a second internal disk on a Mac Pro, but on most Macs the easiest course is to connect an external hard disk, which is what this task assumes.

Configure Time Machine Backups

1 Connect an external USB or FireWire hard disk to your Mac.

● When your Mac recognizes the external hard disk, it adds an icon for the disk to the desktop.

Your Mac asks if you want to use the hard disk as your backup disk.

2 Click **Use as Backup Disk**.

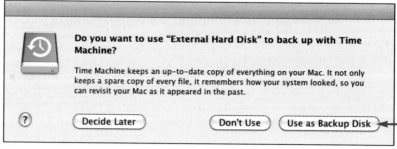

The Time Machine preferences appear.

● This area shows you information about your backups.

③ Click **Close** (🔴).

Note: To make changes to your backup configuration or to examine backup information, click System Preferences (🖥️) in the Dock and then click Time Machine.

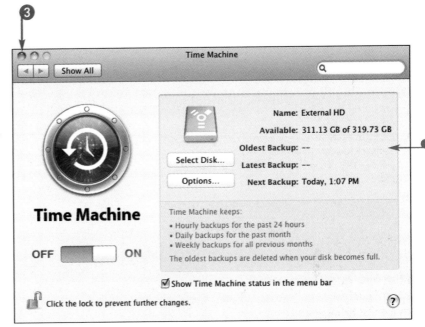

How do Time Machine backups work?

Time Machine makes backing up your Mac easy because backups are handled automatically on the following schedule:

- The initial backup occurs 2 minutes after you configure Time Machine for the first time. This backup includes your entire Mac.

- Time Machine runs another backup every hour. These hourly backups include just those files and folders that you have changed or created since the most recent hourly backup.

- Time Machine runs a daily backup that includes only those files and folders that you have changed or created since the most recent daily backup.

- Time Machine runs a weekly backup that includes only those files and folders that you have changed or created since the most recent weekly backup.

Restore Files Using Time Machine

Because Time Machine makes hourly, daily, and weekly backups, it stores older copies and older versions of your data. You can use these backups to restore any file that you accidentally delete, overwrite, or improperly edit.

Restore Files Using Time Machine

① Click **Finder** (🔲).

② Open the folder you want to restore, or the folder that contains the file you want to restore.

● If you want to restore your entire hard disk, choose **Macintosh HD** in the sidebar.

Note: *Restore your entire hard disk only if your original hard disk crashed and you have had it repaired or replaced.*

③ Click **Time Machine** (⊙).

The Time Machine interface appears.

● Each window represents a backed-up version of the folder.

● This area tells you when the displayed version of the folder was backed up.

● You can use this timeline to navigate the backed-up versions.

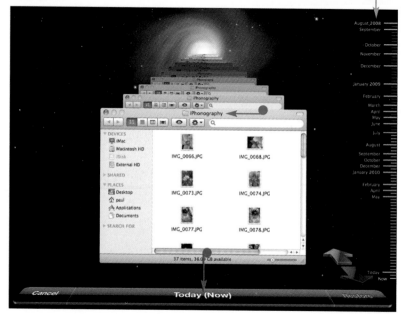

④ Navigate to the date that contains the backup version of the folder or file.

Note: See the tip below to learn how to navigate the Time Machine backups.

⑤ If you are restoring a file, click the file.

⑥ Click **Restore**.

If another version of the folder or file already exists, Time Machine asks if you want to keep it or replace it.

⑦ Click **Replace**.

Time Machine restores the folder or file.

How do I navigate the backups in the Time Machine interface?
Here are the most useful techniques:

- Click the top arrow to jump to the earliest version; click the bottom arrow to return to the most recent version.
- Press and hold the ⌘ key and click the arrows to navigate through the backups one version at a time.
- Use the timeline to click a specific version.
- Click the version windows.

Recondition Your Mac Notebook Battery

To get the most performance out of your Mac notebook's battery, you need to recondition the battery by cycling it. *Cycling* a battery means letting it completely discharge and then fully recharging it again.

To maintain optimal performance, you should cycle your Mac notebook battery once a month or so.

Display the Battery Status Percentage

1. Click the **Battery status** icon (🔋).

2. Click **Show**.

3. Click **Percentage**.

   Your Mac shows the percentage of available battery power remaining.

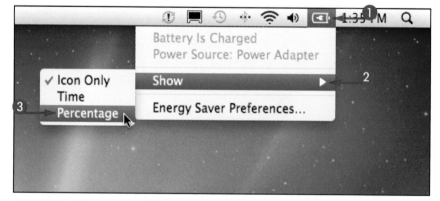

Cycle the Battery

1. Disconnect your Mac notebook's power cord.

● The Battery Status icon changes from 🔋 to 🔋.

② Operate your Mac notebook normally by running applications, working with documents, and so on.

③ As you work, keep your eye on the Battery Status percentage.

When the Battery Status reaches 7%, your Mac warns you that it is now running on reserve power.

④ Click **OK**.

⑤ Reattach the power cord.

You are now running on reserve battery power.

You need to plug the power adapter into your computer and into a power outlet. If you don't, your computer will go to sleep in a few minutes to preserve its memory contents.

OK

Your Mac restarts and the Battery Status icon changes from 🔋 to 🔌.

⑥ Leave your Mac plugged in at least until the Battery Status shows 100%.

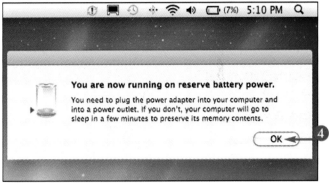

TIPS

I do not see the battery status in my menu bar. How do I display it?

Click **System Preferences** (⚙) in the Dock to open System Preferences, and then click the **Energy Saver** icon. In the Energy Saver window, click **Battery** and then click the **Show battery status in the menu bar** check box (☐ changes to ☑).

Do Mac notebooks suffer from the memory effect?

Older portable computers used rechargeable nickel metal hydride (NiMH) or nickel cadmium (NiCad) batteries. The NiMH and NiCad types were phased out because they can suffer from a problem called the *memory effect*, where the battery loses capacity if you repeatedly recharge it without first fully discharging it. All the latest Mac notebooks have rechargeable lithium-ion (Li-ion) or lithium-polymer (Li-Po) batteries. These batteries are lighter and last longer than NiMH and NiCad batteries and, most importantly, do not suffer from the memory effect.

Troubleshooting Your Mac

Your Mac is a solid computer, and it should give you many years of dependable performance. However, *all* computers eventually run into problems, and your Mac will likely be no exception. To help you get through these inevitable rough patches, this chapter offers a few tried-and-true troubleshooting techniques.

Restart Your Mac

If a hardware device is having a problem with some system files, it often helps to restart your Mac. By rebooting the computer, you reload the entire system, which is often enough to solve many computer problems.

For a problem device that does not have its own power switch, restarting your Mac might not resolve the problem because the device remains powered up the whole time. You can *power cycle* — **shut down and then restart — such devices as a group by power cycling your Mac.**

Restart Your Mac

Restart Your Mac

1 Click the **Apple** icon (![Apple]).

2 Click **Restart**.

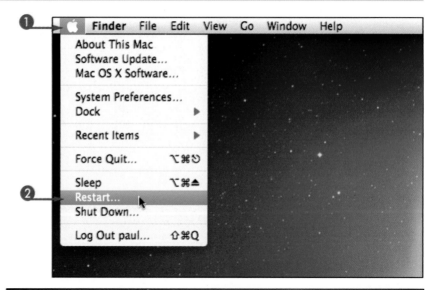

Your Mac asks you to confirm.

3 Click **Restart**.

Note: *To bypass the confirmation dialog, press and hold* Option *when you click the* **Restart** *command.*

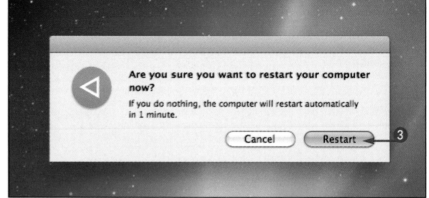

Power Cycle Your Mac

 Click 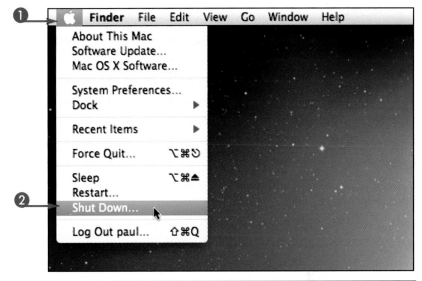.

② Click **Shut Down**.

Your Mac asks you to confirm.

Note: *To bypass the confirmation dialog, hold down* Option *when you click **Shut Down**.*

③ Click **Shut Down**.

④ Wait for 30 seconds to give all devices time to spin down.

⑤ Turn your Mac back on.

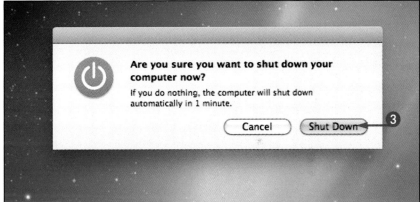

TIP

What other basic troubleshooting techniques can I use?

- Make sure that each device is turned on, that cable connections are secure, and that insertable devices (such as USB devices) are properly inserted.

- If a device is battery powered, replace the batteries.

- If a device has an on/off switch, power cycle the device by turning it off, waiting a few seconds for it to stop spinning, and then turning it back on again.

- Close all running programs.

- Log out of your Mac — click ; click **Log Out *User***, where *User* is your Mac username; and then click **Log Out** — and then log back in again.

Troubleshooting
✓ Check connections
✓ Replace batteries
· Power cycle
✓ Close programs
· Log out

Unlock System Preferences

When you open System Preferences and click an icon, you may find that some or all of the controls in the resulting preferences window are disabled. To enable those controls, you need to unlock the preferences.

Remember that having locked system preferences is not a glitch. Instead, it is a security feature designed to prevent unauthorized users from making changes to sensitive system settings.

① Click **System Preferences** (🖥) in the Dock.

The System Preferences window appears.

② Click the icon of the system preferences you want to work with (such as Parental Controls, as shown here).

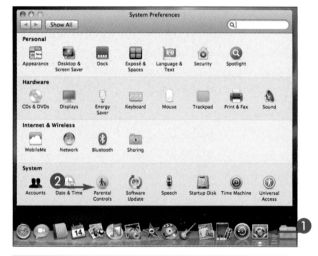

The Parental Controls preferences appear.

③ Click the **System Preferences Locked** icon (🔒).

System Preferences prompts you for an administrator's username and password.

④ Use the Name text box to type the name of an administrator account on your Mac.

⑤ Use the Password text box to type the administrator account's password.

⑥ Click **OK**.

● 🔒 changes to 🔓.

● Your Mac enables the preferences.

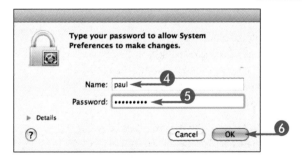

TIPS

Some preferences are already unlocked. Should I lock them?

The purpose behind locking system preferences is to prevent unauthorized changes to those preferences. If you are the only person who uses your Mac, then you do not need to worry about this, so you can leave those other system preferences unlocked for convenience. However, if other people have access to your Mac, you should probably lock important system preferences by clicking 🔓 (which changes to 🔒).

Is there a way to lock my entire Mac?

Yes, you can configure your Mac to require a password when it wakes up from sleep mode or from the screen saver. Click **System Preferences** (🖼) in the Dock, click **Security**, click 🔒, and then type a password. Click **General**, and then click **Require password immediately after sleep or screen saver begins** (☐ changes to ☑).

Force a Stuck Program to Close

When you are working with an application, you may find that it becomes unresponsive and you cannot quit the program normally. In that case, you can tell your Mac to force the program to quit.

When you force a program to quit, you lose any unsaved changes in your open documents. Make sure the program really is stuck before forcing it to quit. See the second tip on the following page for more information.

Force a Stuck Program to Close

① Click **🍎**.

② Click **Force Quit**.

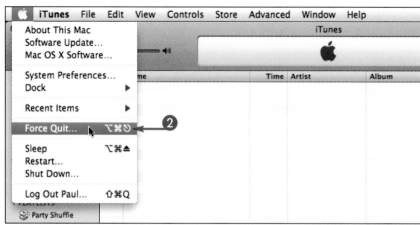

The Force Quit Applications window appears.

③ Click the application you want to shut down.

④ Click **Force Quit**.

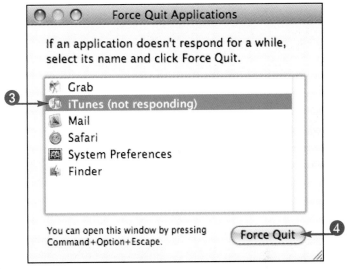

Force Quit Applications

If an application doesn't respond for a while, select its name and click Force Quit.

- Grab
- iTunes (not responding)
- Mail
- Safari
- System Preferences
- Finder

You can open this window by pressing Command+Option+Escape.   **Force Quit**

Your Mac asks you to confirm that you want to force the program to quit.

⑤ Click **Force Quit**.

Your Mac shuts down the program.

⑥ Click **Close** (⬤) to close the Force Quit Applications window.

Force Quit Applications

Do you want to force iTunes to quit?

You will lose any unsaved changes.

Cancel   **Force Quit**

Safari
System Preferences
Finder

You can open this window by pressing Command+Option+Escape.   **Force Quit**

TIPS

Are there easier ways to run the Force Quit command?

Yes. From the keyboard, you can run the Force Quit command by pressing Option + ⌘ + Esc. If the application has a Dock icon, press and hold Control + Option and then click the application's Dock icon. In the menu that appears, click **Force Quit**.

If an application is not responding, does that always mean the program is stuck?

Not necessarily. For example, some program operations — such as recalculating a large spreadsheet or rendering a 3-D image — can take minutes, and during that time the program can appear stuck. Similarly, your Mac may be low on memory, which can also cause a program to seem stuck. In this case, try shutting down some of your other programs to free up some memory.

Repair a Corrupt Preferences File

One of the most common causes of application instability is a preferences file that has somehow become corrupted. You can solve the problem by deleting the preferences file so that the application has to rebuild it.

The downside to this method is that you may have to reconfigure the application's preferences.

① If the problem application is still running, shut it down.

Note: *If you have trouble closing the application, see the section "Force a Stuck Program to Close."*

② Click **Finder** ( ).

③ Click your user account folder.

④ Open the Library folder.

The Library folder appears.

⑤ Open the Preferences folder.

The Preferences folder appears.

6 Click and drag the problem application's preferences file and drop it on the trash.

Note: *See the Tip below to learn how to locate the correct preferences file.*

Your Mac deletes the preferences file.

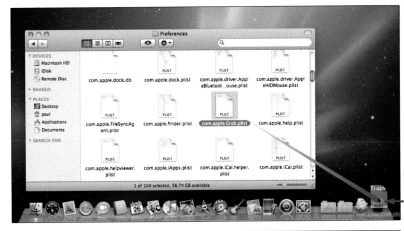

7 Run the application and set some preferences.

● The application creates a new preferences file.

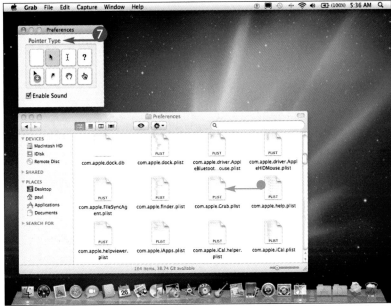

What is a preferences file?
A *preferences file* is a document that stores a user's options, settings, and other data related to a particular application. To specify preferences, click the application's name in the menu bar and then click **Preferences**. The application displays a dialog that you use to specify the preferences. When you are done, the application saves the new settings in the preferences file.

How can I tell which preferences file belongs to the problem application?
Most preferences files use the .plist filename extension. In most cases, the filename uses the following general format: com.*company.application*.plist. Here, *company* is the name of the software company that makes the application, and *application* is the name of the program. Here are some examples: com.apple.iTunes.plist; com.microsoft.Word.plist; com.palm.HotSync.plist.

Reset a Forgotten Password

If you forget the password associated with your Mac OS X main user account, you will be unable to log on to that account and to perform activities such as updating your Mac. You can recover from this problem by resetting the administrative password.

To reset your Mac OS X administrative password, you need to have the original installation DVD that came with your Mac or that you used to install Mac OS X.

Reset a Forgotten Password

① Insert the Mac OS X Installation DVD.

② Restart your Mac.

③ Press and hold **C** while your Mac is restarting.

*Note: You can release **C** when you see the Apple logo.*

The Mac OS X screen appears.

④ Click the language you want to use.

⑤ Click **Continue** (⊙).

The Mac OS X Installer appears.

⑥ Click **Utilities**.

⑦ Click **Reset Password**.

The Reset Password dialog appears.

⑧ Click **Macintosh HD**.

⑨ Click ⊕ and then click your Mac's main user account.

⑩ Type the new password.

⑪ Retype the new password.

⑫ Type a password hint.

⑬ Click **Save**.

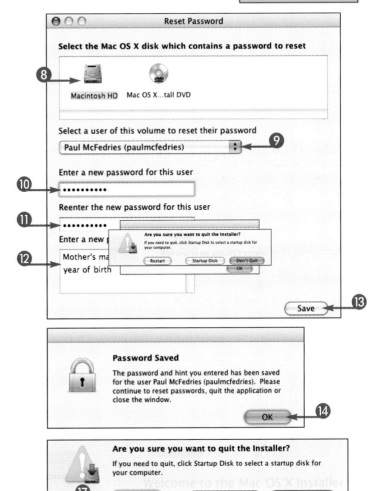

⑭ Click **OK**.

⑮ Press ⌘+Q.

Reset Password quits and returns you to Mac OS X Installer.

⑯ Press ⌘+Q.

Installer asks you to confirm you want to quit.

⑰ Click **Restart**.

Your Mac restarts with your new password in effect.

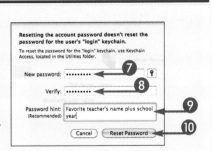

How do I reset passwords for my Mac's other accounts?

① Log in to your Mac using the main administrative account.

② Click **System Preferences** (🖼) in the Dock.

③ Click **Accounts**.

④ Click 🔒, type your administrative password, and click **OK**.

⑤ Click the user account.

⑥ Click **Reset Password**.

⑦ Type the new password.

⑧ Retype the new password.

⑨ Type a password hint.

⑩ Click **Reset Password**.

Repair Disk Permissions

If the permissions on one or more of your Mac's system files become corrupted, your Mac may freeze, run slowly, or become unstable. You can sometimes solve these problems by repairing your Mac's disk permissions.

1. Click **Finder** (■).

2. Click **Applications**.

3. Open the Utilities folder.

Note: You can also open the Utilities folder by pressing Shift + ⌘ + U .

The Utilities folder opens.

4. Double-click **Disk Utility**.

The Disk Utility window appears.

⑤ Click your Mac's hard disk.

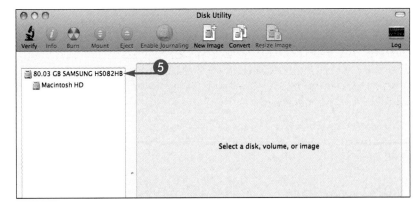

⑥ Click **First Aid**.

⑦ Click **Repair Disk Permissions**.

Your Mac repairs the disk permissions.

⑧ When the repair is complete, press ⌘ + Q to quit Disk Utility.

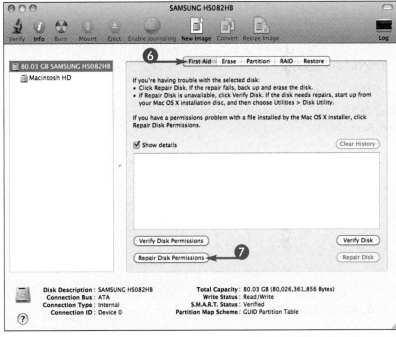

What are disk permissions?
All the files on your Mac have *permissions* associated with them. Permissions are a collection of settings that determine what users or groups of users can do with each file. For example, if read-only permissions apply to a file, it means that all users can only read the contents of the file and cannot make any changes to the file or delete it. If the permissions for your Mac's system files change or get corrupted, it can cause all kinds of problems, including program lock-ups and unstable system behavior.

How do I repair permissions if I cannot start my Mac?
Corrupt disk permissions might prevent your Mac from booting. In this case, follow Steps **1** to **6** in the "Reset a Forgotten Password" section, click **Disk Utility**, and then follow Steps **5** to **7** in this section.

If your Mac will not start, or if an application freezes, an error on the main hard disk is possibly causing the problem. To see if this is the case, you can try repairing the hard disk using the Disk Utility program.

To repair your Mac's main hard drive, you need to have the original installation DVD that came with your Mac or that you used to install Mac OS X.

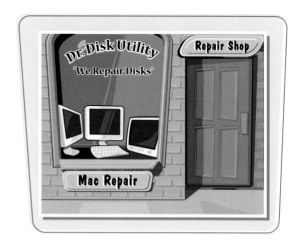

Repair a Disk

1️⃣ Insert the Mac OS X Installation DVD.

2️⃣ Restart your Mac.

3️⃣ Press and hold **C** while your Mac is restarting.

Note: *You can release* **C** *when you see the Apple logo.*

The Mac OS X screen appears.

4️⃣ Click the language you want to use.

5️⃣ Click **Continue** (•••).

The Mac OS X Installer appears.

6️⃣ Click **Utilities**.

7️⃣ Click **Disk Utility**.

The Disk Utility window appears.

8 Click your Mac's hard disk.

9 Click **First Aid**.

10 Click **Repair Disk**.

Disk Utility verifies the hard disk and attempts to repair any errors it finds.

● Information on the disk checks appears here.

● The result of the checks appears here.

11 Press ⌘+Q.

Disk Utility quits and returns you to Mac OS X Installer.

12 Press ⌘+Q.

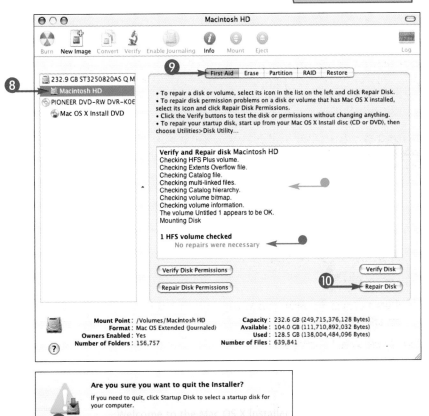

Installer asks you to confirm.

13 Click **Restart**.

Are you sure you want to quit the Installer?

If you need to quit, click Startup Disk to select a startup disk for your computer.

Restart Startup Disk Don't Quit

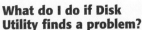

TIPS

How do I repair errors on a secondary hard disk?

If you are working with your Mac's startup hard disk, you must boot to the Mac OS X Install DVD to repair that disk. For all other hard disks, however, you can perform the repair without rebooting. Click **Finder** (⬛), click **Applications**, click **Utilities**, and then double-click **Disk Utility**. Click the disk you want to repair, click **First Aid**, and then click **Repair Disk**.

What do I do if Disk Utility finds a problem?

In the best-case scenario, Disk Utility reports either "No repairs were necessary" or "The volume Macintosh HD appears to be OK." Otherwise, Disk Utility attempts to fix any errors it finds. If Disk Utility cannot fix the errors, you must turn to a third-party disk repair application. Two useful tools are DiskWarrior (www.alsoft.com) and TechTool Pro (www.micromat.com).

Reinstall Mac OS X

If worse comes to worst and your Mac will not start or if your system is completely unstable, then you need to reinstall the operating system.

To reinstall Mac OS X, you need to have the original installation DVD that came with your Mac or that you used to install Mac OS X.

Reinstall Mac OS X

① Insert the Mac OS X Installation DVD.

② Restart your Mac.

③ Press and hold **C** while your Mac is restarting.

Note: *You can release* **C** *when you see the Apple logo.*

The Mac OS X screen appears.

④ Click the language you want to use.

⑤ Click **Continue** ([●]).

The Mac OS X Installer appears.

⑥ Click **Continue**.

The Software License Agreement
dialog appears.

7 Click **Continue**.

*Note: In some versions of the Installer, you click
Agree instead, and then skip Step 8.*

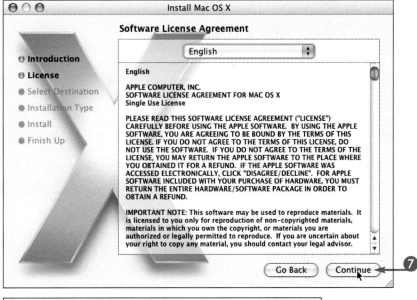

The Installer asks if you agree to
the license terms.

8 Click **Agree**.

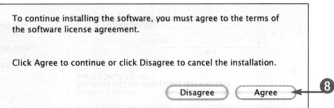

TIPS

**Under what
circumstances should
I reinstall Mac OS X?**

The most common scenario
is when your Mac does not
start, and repairing the hard
disk as described in the
previous section has no
effect. Another common
scenario is when your Mac suffers from frequent
lockups, application crashes, and other unstable
behavior, and repairing preferences files and disk
permissions, as described earlier in this chapter,
have no effect.

**Do I need to back
up my data before
reinstalling?**

No, this is not usually
necessary. The Mac OS X
Installer comes with an
Archive and Install option
that enables you to
preserve your Mac's
existing user accounts as well as each account's
folders. This enables you to use your existing
accounts and data with the reinstalled version of
OS X. However, this option may be disabled if your
Mac does not have enough free hard disk space.

The fastest way to reinstall Mac OS X is to perform the installation using the Archive and Install option. This not only preserves your user accounts and data, but it also bypasses the Setup Assistant, which greatly reduces the number of steps.

The Select a Destination dialog appears.

9 Click your Mac's main hard disk.

10 Click **Options**.

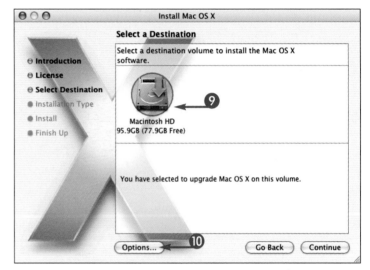

The installation options appear.

11 Click **Archive and Install** (⊙ changes to ⊙).

12 Click **Preserve Users and Network Settings** (☐ changes to ☑).

13 Click **OK**.

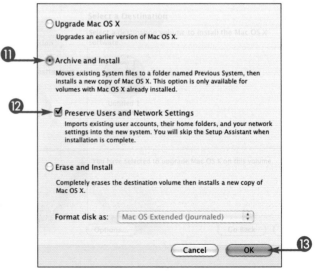

14 Click **Continue**.

14

15 Click **Install**.

Installer reinstalls Mac OS X on your Mac.

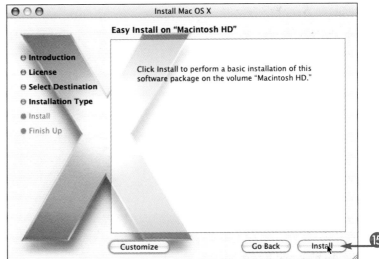

15

TIPS

Why does my Apple Bluetooth mouse not work with the Installer program?

The Mac OS X Installer application does not come with the necessary device drivers to work with the signals that the Apple Bluetooth mouse or any other wireless mouse generates. You cannot reinstall Mac OS X unless your Mac has a mouse that is physically connected to the computer.

Once Mac OS X is reinstalled, what else do I need to do?

The first thing you should do is restore your Mac from your most recent Time Machine backup. If you have no backup, you should update your Mac's software. To do this, click ⬛ and then click **Software Update**. Next, you should reinstall any third-party applications that you used on your old Mac OS X installation. Once you have your applications installed, you should check your preferences in each program to make sure they are configured correctly.

Index

Index

Index

Index

Index

Index

Read Less–Learn More®

Visual®

There's a Visual book
for every learning level...

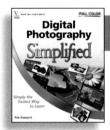

Simplified®

The place to start if you're new to computers. Full color.

- Computers
- Creating Web Pages
- Digital Photography
- Internet
- Mac OS
- Office
- Windows

Teach Yourself VISUALLY™

Get beginning to intermediate-level training in a variety of topics. Full color.

- Access
- Bridge
- Chess
- Computers
- Crocheting
- Digital Photography
- Dog training
- Dreamweaver
- Excel
- Flash
- Golf
- Guitar
- Handspinning
- HTML
- iLife
- iPhoto
- Jewelry Making & Beading
- Knitting
- Mac OS
- Office
- Photoshop
- Photoshop Elements
- Piano
- Poker
- PowerPoint
- Quilting
- Scrapbooking
- Sewing
- Windows
- Wireless Networking
- Word

Top 100 Simplified® Tips & Tricks

Tips and techniques to take your skills beyond the basics. Full color.

- Digital Photography
- eBay
- Excel
- Google
- Internet
- Mac OS
- Office
- Photoshop
- Photoshop Elements
- PowerPoint
- Windows

...all designed for visual learners—just like you!